READINGS ON

ALL QUIET ON THE WESTERN FRONT

OTHER TITLES IN THE GREENHAVEN PRESS LITERARY COMPANION SERIES:

AMERICAN AUTHORS

Maya Angelou
Stephen Crane
Emily Dickinson
William Faulkner
F. Scott Fitzgerald
Nathaniel Hawthorne
Ernest Hemingway
Herman Melville
Arthur Miller
Eugene O'Neill
Edgar Allan Poe
John Steinbeck
Mark Twain
Thornton Wilder

AMERICAN LITERATURE

The Adventures of
  Huckleberry Finn
The Adventures of Tom
  Sawyer
The Catcher in the Rye
The Crucible
Death of a Salesman
The Glass Menagerie
The Grapes of Wrath
The Great Gatsby
Of Mice and Men
The Old Man and the Sea
The Pearl
The Scarlet Letter
A Separate Peace

BRITISH AUTHORS

Jane Austen
Joseph Conrad
Charles Dickens

BRITISH LITERATURE

Animal Farm
The Canterbury Tales
Great Expectations
Hamlet
Julius Caesar
Lord of the Flies
Macbeth
Pride and Prejudice
Romeo and Juliet
Shakespeare: The Comedies
Shakespeare: The Histories
Shakespeare: The Sonnets
Shakespeare: The Tragedies
A Tale of Two Cities
Wuthering Heights

WORLD AUTHORS

Fyodor Dostoyevsky
Homer
Sophocles

WORLD LITERATURE

A Doll's House
The Diary of a Young Girl

THE GREENHAVEN PRESS
Literary Companion
TO WORLD LITERATURE

ALL QUIET ON THE WESTERN FRONT

Terry O'Neill, *Book Editor*

David L. Bender, *Publisher*
Bruno Leone, *Executive Editor*
Bonnie Szumski, *Series Editor*

Greenhaven Press, Inc., San Diego, CA

Every effort has been made to trace the owners of copyrighted material. The articles in this volume may have been edited for content, length, and/or reading level. The titles have been changed to enhance the editorial purpose. Those interested in locating the original source will find the complete citation on the first page of each article.

Library of Congress Cataloging-in-Publication Data

Readings on All quiet on the western front / Terry O'Neill, book editor.
    p.   cm. — (The Greenhaven Press literary companion to world literature)
   Includes bibliographical references and index.
   ISBN 1-56510-825-6 (alk. paper). —
ISBN 1-56510-824-8 (pbk. : alk. paper)
   1. Remarque, Erich Maria, 1898–1970. Im Westen nichts Neues. 2. World War, 1914–1918—Literature and the war. I. O'Neill, Terry, 1944–   . II. Series.
PT2635.E68I625   1999
833'.912—dc21   98-33585
                                    CIP

Cover photo: Photofest

Copyright ©1999 by Greenhaven Press, Inc.
PO Box 289009
San Diego, CA 92198-9009
Printed in the U.S.A.

"This book is to be neither an accusation nor a confession, and least of all an adventure, for death is not an adventure to those who stand face to face with it. It will try simply to tell of a generation of men who, even though they may have escaped its shells, were destroyed by the war."

—*Erich Maria Remarque,*
All Quiet on the Western Front

CONTENTS

Chapter 1: The Voice of a Generation

Chapter 2: A Work of Art

FOREWORD

*"'Tis the good reader that
makes the good book."*

Ralph Waldo Emerson

The story's bare facts are simple: The captain, an old and scarred seafarer, walks with a peg leg made of whale ivory. He relentlessly drives his crew to hunt the world's oceans for the great white whale that crippled him. After a long search, the ship encounters the whale and a fierce battle ensues. Finally the captain drives his harpoon into the whale, but the harpoon line catches the captain about the neck and drags him to his death.

A simple story, a straightforward plot—yet, since the 1851 publication of Herman Melville's *Moby-Dick*, readers and critics have found many meanings in the struggle between Captain Ahab and the whale. To some, the novel is a cautionary tale that depicts how Ahab's obsession with revenge leads to his insanity and death. Others believe that the whale represents the unknowable secrets of the universe and that Ahab is a tragic hero who dares to challenge fate by attempting to discover this knowledge. Perhaps Melville intended Ahab as a criticism of Americans' tendency to become involved in well-intentioned but irrational causes. Or did Melville model Ahab after himself, letting his fictional character express his anger at what he perceived as a cruel and distant god?

Although literary critics disagree over the meaning of *Moby-Dick*, readers do not need to choose one particular interpretation in order to gain an understanding of Melville's novel. Instead, by examining various analyses, they can gain numerous insights into the issues that lie under the surface of the basic plot. Studying the writings of literary critics can also aid readers in making their own assessments of *Moby-Dick* and other literary works and in developing analytical thinking skills.

The Greenhaven Literary Companion Series was created with these goals in mind. Designed for young adults, this unique anthology series provides an engaging and comprehensive introduction to literary analysis and criticism. The essays included in the Literary Companion Series are chosen for their accessibility to a young adult audience and are expertly edited in consideration of both the reading and comprehension levels of this audience. In addition, each essay is introduced by a concise summation that presents the contributing writer's main themes and insights. Every anthology in the Literary Companion Series contains a varied selection of critical essays that cover a wide time span and express diverse views. Wherever possible, primary sources are represented through excerpts from authors' notebooks, letters, and journals and through contemporary criticism.

Each title in the Literary Companion Series pays careful consideration to the historical context of the particular author or literary work. In-depth biographies and detailed chronologies reveal important aspects of authors' lives and emphasize the historical events and social milieu that influenced their writings. To facilitate further research, every anthology includes primary and secondary source bibliographies of articles and/or books selected for their suitability for young adults. These engaging features make the Greenhaven Literary Companion series ideal for introducing students to literary analysis in the classroom or as a library resource for young adults researching the world's great authors and literature.

Exceptional in its focus on young adults, the Greenhaven Literary Companion Series strives to present literary criticism in a compelling and accessible format. Every title in the series is intended to spark readers' interest in leading American and world authors, to help them broaden their understanding of literature, and to encourage them to formulate their own analyses of the literary works that they read. It is the editors' hope that young adult readers will find these anthologies to be true companions in their study of literature.

INTRODUCTION

The students, led by Professor Bäumler, marched through the streets of Berlin with their musical accompaniment and carts full of "decadent" books to be burned. Around eleven o'clock they arrived at the partly cordoned off Opera Square and threw their torches onto the pyre that had been erected in the center. As the flames leapt up, students formed a human chain to pass the books from hand to hand, and soon the first of more than twenty thousand volumes were consumed by the fire. The crowd cheered wildly and then listened to a brief speech by one of the student leaders.

Then while brass bands of the SA and SS played rousing march music, nine representatives of the student body took turns throwing books into the flames. They had been assigned specific subject areas and authors, and as they added their share to the bonfire they cried [a condemnation of each author. Remarque's detractor yelled]:

"Against literary betrayal of the soldiers of the World War, for the education of the people in the spirit of truthfulness! I surrender to the flames the writings of Erich Maria Remarque."[1]

Such was the fate of one of the most famous novels of the early twentieth century in the land of its author's birth. Published in 1929, ten years after the end of the Great War, *All Quiet on the Western Front* was the first best-seller of Erich Maria Remarque's career. Aided by an aggressive marketing campaign by its publisher, the novel was greeted with enthusiasm in much of the world. Although the exact figures are debated today, *All Quiet* sold in the neighborhood of 1.5 million copies outside of Germany in its first year and nearly a million copies in Germany, and it was translated into thirty or more languages. Yet by 1933, the National Socialists (Nazis) had gained power in Germany and condemned the book, its author, and many other works that seemed to them to be treasonous, or at least not to be in the right spirit for the new Germany. The book burning described above happened

1. Egbert Krispyn, *Anti-Nazi Writers in Exile.* Athens: University of Georgia Press, 1978.

in May 1933, three months after the National Socialists had swept political elections and were moving Germany once again in the direction of war.

What was the treason committed by Remarque? It was his audacious portrait of war as inglorious and of young German soldiers suffering and dying almost meaninglessly instead of victoriously battling for their country. The Nazis felt the novel would encourage people to avoid war rather than enthusiastically and romantically fight for the Fatherland.

Despite its controversial nature, the original publication date could not have been better timed to achieve success. In the years immediately following World War I, people did not want to confront the experiences of that terrible time. Soldiers of all nations found it difficult to return home to normal lives after the traumatic events they had lived through, events that included watching their friends die in battle. But by 1929, many of them were ready at last to face the experience of war. A spate of war memoirs and war novels was published during the late 1920s and early 1930s, and Remarque's was the most widely read of all of them. One authority, bibliographer C.R. Owen, says that in its entire publishing history, *All Quiet* has sold more copies than any other book except the Bible.

All Quiet combined lyrical and straightforward writing in a way that seemed to perfectly explain the war experience to those who had lived through it as well as those who had been at home, and, unlike most previous war novels, it did not glamorize war. *All Quiet* showed war in all its mundane and boring, filthy and terrifying aspects. The young soldiers who are the focus of the novel do have their moments of patriotism and valor, but for the most part, readers see their daily lives in the trenches as they were really lived. Few people who read the novel can come away unmoved by the young men's experiences and by war's horrifying futility.

The characters are mere boys when they are drafted, but most of them come to military service with the idea that they will serve their country bravely and heroically. Their romantic views are sorely challenged, however, by harsh training, often brutal officers, tedious waiting in the trenches, bad and inadequate food, and lack of privacy. One of the few good things they seem to gain—if they survive—is their friendship with their fellows. They become totally committed to and dependent on the men with whom they serve.

Although Remarque's characters are German, he clearly

portrays the life of the ordinary soldier worldwide. His perfect depiction struck home with soldiers and nonsoldiers in
Germany and around the globe.

Hollywood's Universal Studios immediately turned the
novel into a powerful film and made the career of its young,
unknown star, Lew Ayres. It opened to rave reviews in late
1930, and thousands of moviegoers crowded to see it. In Germany, however, many of the country's political leaders—Fas-
cists, militarists, and Centrists—tried to ban the film. Failing
that, Hermann Goebbels, later the propaganda minister of
the Nazi Party, arranged violent demonstrations that pan-
icked moviegoers. Remarque stated:

> Outside, before the theatre the Brownshirts stood at attention,
> awaiting my arrival with screams. What was remarkable:
> none of the Brown ones was probably over 19; children
> protested against my version of the war, not having them-
> selves experienced it. . . . Later on, Goebbels sent me an ulti-
> matum, according to which I was to declare that the Jews Ull-
> stein [his publisher] and Lämmle (in Hollywood) [Universal
> Studio's head and the movie's producer] had been exclusively
> responsible for the film—which, by the way, coincided exactly
> with the truth. . . . Goebbels would then leave me alone, pro-
> nounce me the Aryan of the future, and celebrate me as a vic-
> tim. I rejected that.

The film later was banned in Germany, Austria, and other
countries under Fascist control. The book, too, was banned in
several countries. And by 1933, Remarque, harassed by the
Nazis, had left Germany. He would not return again until 1952.

All Quiet on the Western Front has been republished hundreds of times in the seventy-some years since its first appearance. It led Remarque to being recommended as a can-
didate for the Nobel Peace Prize, but German protest knocked
him out of consideration. It has sold an estimated 50 million
copies, and two more film versions of the novel have been
made. Without question, the novel, Remarque's best, has had
a tremendous impact.

This Literary Companion explores the book's influence
and meaning. The essays are written by literary critics, pro-
fessors, war veterans, and Remarque himself and span several decades. Despite the great and lasting impact of *All
Quiet,* comparatively little has been written about it or its author, especially in English. The essays in this collection rep-
resent some of the more interesting commentary available.

This volume also includes brief exploratory introductions
to each article, subheads, and brief quotations from addi-

tional sources, all aimed at aiding the reader in gleaning key points from their reading. A biographical introduction to Erich Maria Remarque and a detailed chronology help put the author and the novel into the context of their times. An annotated bibliography suggests additional works for the reader who wants to learn more about Remarque, his world, and *All Quiet on the Western Front.*

Considered one of the best writers of twentieth-century Germany (only Thomas Mann and Heinrich Böll are judged greater), Erich Maria Remarque is quite possibly the most accessible and the best known. His classic *All Quiet on the Western Front* has sold millions of copies since its first publication and continues to be taught in classrooms. Nearly all of his other novels were best-sellers in their time.

All Quiet has become perhaps the most widely read anti-war novel because readers can identify with its lyrically and realistically depicted theme. Charles W. Hoffmann says that Remarque's books "are generally well-crafted novels with clear plot lines; they are easy to read; and they mix adventure, suspense, social comment, and some violence with a central love story." They are "documents of their age, . . . vividly chronicling at least one side of the German experience in this momentous century . . . and his episodic style and his use of the first person and the present tense [give] . . . the appearance of eyewitness authenticity."

Remarque once said that "there is nothing worse for an author than that his first book should become an international success," and, indeed, this was true for him. *All Quiet* was a phenomenal success, and all of his following books were compared to it, both for their writing and for their track records. As C.R. Owen points out, all of Remarque's books after *All Quiet* were "found wanting. And every one of them was given little prospect of ever becoming popular, and every one of them sold at least 100,000 copies."

Erich Maria Remarque, not exactly a "man of the people" himself, managed to write an enduring work that speaks to readers of all ages, genders, and nationalities, and it is for this feat that he will be remembered.

ERICH MARIA REMARQUE:
A BIOGRAPHY

"I am opposed to anything autobiographical and biographical. . . . What I have learned in my life, I have used in my works and the rest is private and does not influence the work and this is how I would like to keep it." So said Erich Maria Remarque in 1969 when his old school friend Hanns-Gerd Rabe asked for information in preparation for writing a biography of the author. Unfortunately for those who want to know more about the man, this was Remarque's attitude from the moment he first attained fame, with the publication of *All Quiet on the Western Front* in 1929.

Because of his own reticence about discussing his life and the deliberate misinformation spread by his enemies, many of the important events in Remarque's life, particularly in the early years, remain unknown or shadowed by controversy. For example, when the National Socialists in Germany were trying to discredit Remarque, some writers stated that he was not a true German but a Hungarian Jew whose actual family name was Kramer. This inaccuracy continued to appear in published reports about Remarque even after his death. In actuality, Remarque was born Erich Paul Remark in Osnabrück, Germany, in 1898. Some of his French ancestors used the surname Remarque, and this is where the name he is known by today originated.

"THE BEST ONE"

Erich's parents were the rather dour and undemonstrative Peter Franz Remark, a bookbinder, and Anna Maria Stallknecht Remark, a woman who devoted much of her attention to her first child, Theo, who was three when Erich was born. Theo died when Erich was only three years old. When Anna came home from Theo's burial, she told Erich that now he would have to be "the best one." Erich, resentful that he had been second in his mother's affections, angrily struck her, an act that guiltily remained in his memory for the rest of his life.

Peter and Anna Maria also had two daughters, Erna, born in 1900, and Elfreide, born in 1903. Little is known of the details of their lives.

The Remarks were not a wealthy family. They moved frequently to save money, but they always stayed within the same general area of the small city. Erich knew its nooks and crannies well, and Osnabrück is the setting of many scenes in his writing. Erich's many interests as a young boy included stamp and butterfly collecting, magic tricks, games, music, and books. A number of the characters in his novels share these fascinations.

The family was staunchly Catholic, and Erich and his sisters attended Catholic grade school. At the time, young people in Osnabrück could not expect to be educated beyond eighth grade if the family did not have enough money to send them to private school. The only way for Erich to continue his education was to go to a teacher training school, which was free. Consequently, Erich attended the Präparande from about age fourteen to seventeen, preparing to teach in Catholic elementary schools.

THE DREAM CIRCLE

Always something of an iconoclast, Erich became involved in a literary circle when he was a teenager. The group of mostly young men and women was mentored by thirty-six-year-old Fritz Hörstemeier, a poet and painter. The members of the group, *Die Traumbude* (the Dream Circle), dressed in a sophisticated and bohemian manner, wrote poetry and lavishly romantic prose, and discussed great ideas, literature, sex, and the sad state of society. This group, in a sense, became Erich's family. He had always felt that he did not receive intellectual stimulation or encouragement from his parents, but in this group, he found his soulmates. With these people he could be the intellectual and artist he romantically envisioned himself to be. He could write, paint, play music, and be appreciated for his talents. At home, his father frowned upon such frivolity and encouraged Erich to be practical, and his mother was somewhat distant.

Erich was considered a handsome young man, "with large bones on a medium frame, the same wide, fair brow [as his mother], clear blue eyes, and sensuous mouth," reports biographer Julie Gilbert. Even as a young man and something of an outsider, Erich was attractive to women—a trait he retained throughout his life. Remarque attributed this to his family life.

He remarked to his friend Hanns-Gerd Rabe in 1971 that he had always had to work hard to develop friendships with men, but "with women it always came naturally." Growing up, it was his sisters and mother with whom he interacted the most. He felt he had little in common with his father. Consequently, he always felt more comfortable with women.

Erich's first love, Erika Haase, was also a member of the Dream Circle. Erich's diaries from this time are filled with lyrical descriptions of Erika and his feelings for her.

In 1915, Erich's mother was diagnosed with cancer. For the two short remaining years of her life, she suffered intermittent debilitating bouts of illness because of the disease.

WAR

During this time a number of Erich's friends and acquaintances had joined the army or been drafted. Germany was a major player in the Great War. Erich, preoccupied with his artistic pursuits, avoided the army as long as he could, but in 1916 he received his draft notice. After rigorous training he was sent to the western front—France. Erich was part of a sapper, or engineering, unit that laid barbed wire and built gun emplacements, bunkers, and dugouts.

On July 31, 1917, the first day of the Battle of Flanders, a five-month slaughter in which almost three-quarters of a million British, French, and German soldiers became casualties, Erich was seriously wounded. He was struck in the neck, the left leg above the knee, and the right forearm. He was sent to St. Vincenz Hospital in Duisburg, Germany. There he spent a fairly pleasant recovery period, flirting with the hospital administrator's daughter, writing, and convalescing. He submitted several pieces of poetry and short prose to *Die Schönheit,* an avant-garde German journal, and also began his first novel, *Die Traumbude,* a romantic and sentimental work based on his Dream Circle. He was released from the hospital on October 13, 1918, and reported back to the service. On November 7 the battalion physician pronounced him fit for duty, but Erich did not have to return to battle because the armistice was signed on November 11, ending the war.

Much later Erich told editor Frédéric Lefèvre,

> At that time I was brimming over with enthusiasm and animated, as all young Germans were, by a great feeling of patriotism. We were fighting for the salvation of the world and the salvation of civilization. I am now quite convinced that young Englishmen and young Frenchmen thought the same thing. But afterward, afterward! The war was too terrible and too

long for me not to learn to think otherwise. After it was all over
I saw all its hideousness, but there was one thing I could not
accept; I saw my best friend lying in the mud, his abdomen
torn open. That is what is really insupportable and incomprehensible and what is no less comprehensible is that it required
so many post-war years and so much reflection for me to realize the full atrocity of these occurrences.

Because of his service in the German army, many people
assumed that the war novel Remarque wrote more than a
decade later was autobiographical. But such was not the case.
Like many writers, he based some characters and events on
people he knew and things that happened to him or to people
he knew, but he fictionalized them. When *All Quiet* was published, some critics of the book, including at least one person
who had served with him, complained that he had distorted
things, made things up, or told things that were not true. Remarque was the first to admit this; he had written a novel, not
a memoir. Hanns-Gerd Rabe wrote that "the most difficult
time to describe in R.'s life is his time as a soldier, because reality and fiction in his novel *All Quiet*... often overlap, despite
the fact that the novel does not portray R.'s war experiences;
however, he does use the reality of war in its brutality."

AFTER THE WAR

After the war Erich returned to teacher training. Many of the
veterans who returned to school were angry at being treated
like naive and inexperienced seventeen-year-olds. In reality,
they were now men who had gone through all the initiations
one should need to be treated as adults. Erich became the
spokesperson for Catholic veterans in teacher training and
Hanns-Gerd Rabe, who was to become a lifelong friend, was
the spokesperson for Protestant veterans. They rebelled against
the school authorities and prevailed in making reforms.

Erich also returned to his dandified ways of Die Traumbude. He was often seen wearing dress military uniforms
with medals (not all of which he was entitled to) and a monocle and carrying a quirt. At other times he was impeccably
dressed in the latest styles. Erich believed that people judged
others by their appearance, and he was determined to make a
strong impression. During this time Erich gave piano lessons
to earn money. He contributed some to his family's household
expenses, used some to dress fashionably, and used part to
help finance the publication of his novel *Die Traumbude*. In
later years Erich wrote, "A dreadful book! If I hadn't written
something better later on, this book would be reason enough

to commit suicide." He was not alone in thinking the book dreadful. It was such an embarrassment that when *All Quiet* was published, Ullstein, the publisher, bought all of the copies of *Die Traumbude* he could find and burned them.

Following the completion of his training, Erich taught in a series of outlying villages. His outspokenness and nonconformity frequently got him into trouble. In one town he had a major confrontation with the priest; the two men wrote nasty letters back and forth, the priest withheld part of Erich's salary, and Erich was brought up before a church board and admonished.

Erich gave up teaching after just one year. He could not stand the restrictions, and his ambitions lay in literature. He spent the next two years doing odd jobs—selling tombstones, playing the organ at a mental institution, and traveling around selling shawls and fabric to farm wives. All the while he was sending essays, reviews, and poems to *Die Schönheit* and other publications. In 1922 he got his first "literary" job in Hannover: He was employed in the advertising department at Continental Rubber Company, a distributor of automobile tires and other rubber products. Soon Erich was billing himself as the advertising editor and editor in chief, writing for the *Continental Echo,* a publication put out by the company to promote its products. He wrote adventure stories, advertising ditties, and essays, and he drew cartoons as well. It was during this time that he first began using the name Erich Maria Remarque. ("Maria" may have been taken from his mother's name, or perhaps it was modeled after the famous German poet Rainer Maria Rilke.) He also developed a passion for cars and racing.

Biographer Harley U. Taylor Jr. writes that Remarque enjoyed his Hannover years, in part because of the city's many cultural offerings. Remarque loved to attend cultural and social events and, writes Taylor, "Remarque was a very popular man among the ladies. His blonde good looks, combined with an attitude which could be intriguingly aloof and solitary or boyishly charming and gregarious, made him quite appealing to the women."

As a promoter of Continental products, Remarque had the opportunity to travel, which he thoroughly enjoyed. However, biographer Julie Gilbert writes, "As a single man on the road, he succumbed to two temptations: drinking and prostitutes," two tastes that stayed with him through most of his life. Gilbert says Remarque "had a genuine tenderness for 'women of the night.' He found their reduced circumstances, which they attempted to disguise and embellish, touching and profoundly human." Often he merely spent the night talking to them and treating them to expensive cigarettes, brandy, and meals.

Taylor writes of Remarque, "There is no doubt . . . concerning Remarque's style of travel. He was a man who believed in going first class whenever circumstances permitted. Moreover, he always managed to do it with style and flair. Remarque, the consummate man of the world, established his credentials early, particularly because he was traveling on his employer's money."

In 1925, Remarque met a beautiful and lively young actress and divorceé, Jutta Ilse Ingeborg Ellen Zambona Winkelfhoff. Also in 1925, Remarque was offered a job as picture editor with *Sport im Bild* (*Sports in Pictures*), a sophisticated popular publication that allowed him and Jutta to move to Berlin, where they married. While the two had much in common—both loved the good life—their marriage was certainly not conventional. Each conducted many affairs during the years they lived together, and even after they divorced, remarried, and divorced again, they maintained a symbiotic relationship almost until death.

SPORT IM BILD

Germany's cosmopolitan capital, Berlin, was the perfect place for an ambitious young writer. "The brash vitality of the city and its wide range of intellectual, cultural, and sensual activities were tremendously appealing and stimulating for [Remarque]," reports Harley U. Taylor Jr.

The new job, while not in advertising, was in many ways a continuation of what he had done at Continental. He continued to write about and interact with sports personalities, to travel, and to live an urbane lifestyle. He was thrilled to be able to take trips with auto racer Rudolph Caracciola as part of his job. "A young man in a hurry," as Taylor writes, Remarque actively networked with other Berlin journalists at the favorite restaurants and bars, and he even bought himself a title: He paid an impoverished baron to adopt him. "With his new, if spurious credentials, Remarque, monocle in place, was a striking figure in the lower reaches of Berlin society," Taylor writes. Remarque did not use the title after his masterpiece *All Quiet on the Western Front* made him a success.

Remarque's second novel, *Station am Horizont* (*Station on the Horizon*) was serialized (though never published as a single volume) in *Sport im Bild* in late 1927. It was a car-racing soap opera, described by one friend as an "unpretentious novel with first-class radiators and beautiful women."

To all appearances, young Remarque was a success. He had a glamorous job, a glamorous wife, a glamorous lifestyle, and enough money to enjoy them. Still, some old unhappiness nagged at him. Finally, he sat down and began to write a novel loosely based on his war experiences. In a rare 1929 interview, he said,

> I had never thought about writing on the war before. At the time, it was spring of last year (1928) [and] I was busy with quite different things. I was employed as illustration editor of a magazine. . . . I suffered fairly of attacks of despair. At the attempt to overcome them, I sought out quite consciously and systematically the cause of my depressions. Through this deliberate analysis I hit upon my war experiences. I could detect the same among many acquaintances and friends. All of us were—and often still are—restless, aimless, at times exalted, at times indifferent, but basically quite disenchanted. The shadow of the war hung over us even when we did not think of it at all. On the same day that I hit upon this thought, I began to write, without much premeditation. This went on for six weeks, every evening, when I came home from the office. And then the book was finished.

This, of course, was *All Quiet on the Western Front,* the book he wrote the quickest and that remained his most famous for his entire career. In later years he also called it his first novel, discounting completely *Die Traumbude* and *Station am Horizont.*

All Quiet was rejected by the first publisher that reviewed it, but accepted by the second. It was first serialized in the publisher's own newspaper, *Die Vossiche Zeitung,* and then printed as a hardcover book. The publisher, Ullstein, was confident of the book's marketability and conducted a high-powered publicity campaign. Ullstein sent out press releases and even put a special twenty-one-page advertising supplement in the leading book news publication. The ad supplement recorded the amazing sales the book was achieving and played up the controversy it was arousing, hoping to pique book buyers' curiosity.

As it turned out, Remarque had written the right book at the right time. It was an unprecedented international success. It was purchased by four dozen book clubs, translated into between thirty-five and fifty-five languages, sold 650,000 copies in its first six months ("a success never before achieved by a German novel," noted Remarque archivist Angelika Howind), and was sold to the movies. It was read in schools, by former soldiers and their families (Ullstein's publicity included a letter from a veteran's wife that read, "My husband who had been in the field and twice wounded had never told me any of his front-line experiences. Now he always pushes this book in my hand, saying, 'Here, you can read a truthful description of life at war.'"), by Africans, the English, people in Turkey, and hundreds of thousands of others all over the world.

The book's success was also a source of criticism. While Remarque claimed to have repressed his war experiences until the day he sat down and began writing the book, some critics did not believe him. They said that Remarque, an ambitious young man very familiar with the publishing world, had analyzed the marketplace and set out to write a book people would buy. This is probably not the case. The book appears to be a heartfelt rendering of what it meant to be a foot soldier in the war. Nevertheless, these critics tried to tarnish Remarque's success.

THE RISE OF THE NATIONAL SOCIALISTS

While the book was meeting with astounding success all over the world, in Germany, Remarque's homeland, it was confronting its greatest challenge. Egbert Krispyn, author of *Anti-Nazi Writers in Exile*, notes that the Weimar Republic, established in 1919, was the first attempt to establish a democratic government in Germany. Unfortunately, in part because of Allied restrictions, the government faced difficult hurdles. Egbert writes,

> The peace treaty of Versailles that had been imposed on the Germans contained many unrealistic conditions designed to prevent them from ever again becoming powerful enough to launch another war. But these same stipulations also in effect denied them the chance to reconstruct their country and restore their national self-respect and sense of dignity. This caused very deep and widespread resentment among the population.

When the American stock market crashed in 1929, precipitating the worldwide Great Depression, it was the last straw. The elections of 1930 seated 107 National Socialists, making them the largest party in the country. The National Socialists (also known as Nazis, from a shortening of their German name) were determined to restore Germany's pride and prosperity, even if it meant going to war again. Patriotism and German superiority were their watchwords, and anything that did not enhance their goals was viewed as traitorous, including Remarque's novel.

Although *All Quiet on the Western Front* may not appear to be anti-German to the average reader today, the National Socialists deemed it so. Instead of portraying glorious German soldiers fighting loyally for the Fatherland, it portrayed ordinary young men living in squalor, suffering injuries and death for no apparent purpose, and feeling more boredom and fear than patriotism. The worldwide response to the novel showed how soldiers from other countries identified with the soldiers portrayed in the book, which, to the Nazis, smacked of internationalism rather than the superiority of the German soldier. And the book was seen by many as antiwar, an anathema to the Nazis who viewed war as one way to win back their country's glory.

Ironically, Marxists, who were in favor of internationalism and were against war, also criticized Remarque. Their criticism, however, was that Remarque portrayed the evils of war but he did nothing to stop it in real life. He shunned politics as well as publicity and did not publicly support any cause, even pacifism. Remarque even refused to speak out about Hitler.

(A third branch of criticism argued that since the book was so popular, it couldn't be great literature; it was mere popular pulp.)

The National Socialists managed to ban Remarque's book from German classrooms; when the wildly popular movie was released in 1930, they banned it as well, after first frightening away movie patrons with violent demonstrations.

As a result of the publicity and harrassment Remarque was receiving from the Nazis, he moved back to Osnabrück, seeking the peace he needed to work on his next book. But by 1933 he had left Germany for good. He said at the time that he had simply left the country to be free of distraction, but others said that if he had not fled he would have been imprisoned—or worse. Like many other German refugees, he relocated to Switzerland. In 1931, at the urging of a foresightful mistress, he had bought a villa called Casa Monte Tabor in the small town of Porto Ronco, just above Ascona and overlooking Lake Maggiore. Remarque lived there off and on for the rest of his life. He and Jutta had divorced in 1930, but Jutta soon joined him in Switzerland. She said she felt unsafe living as Remarque's former wife in a country that loathed him.

SUCCESS

The success of *All Quiet* afforded Remarque more money than he had thought possible. In the early months of 1930, his royalties from American sales alone totaled ninety thousand dollars, a huge sum for that time. The money enabled him to live very comfortably and to begin what was to become an outstanding art collection. He did not buy stocks or other conventional financial investments. Instead, he put much of his money in rare Chinese bronzes, paintings by the great French Impressionists, and oriental rugs, all of which greatly appreciated in value over the years. His collection was so fine, in fact, that by the 1940s museums and other collectors often called him for advice. Another thrilling benefit of his success was a gift from his publisher, Ullstein. It was a a Lancia, a sports car that he adored and kept for many years.

In Porto Ronco, Remarque finished the second book in a trilogy dealing with the experience of war and its aftermath. *All Quiet*, the first, shows young men who can only conclude that there is little meaning to existence; whether they live or die has nothing to do with their own skills, or will, or virtue; it seems to be mere chance. *The Road Back*, the second in the trilogy, is a bit more optimistic. When he was working on it, Remarque said, "In my next book, which I am now writing, I describe the way back to life, how a young man like myself—and Paul Bäumer—experienced war as a youth, who still carries its scars, and who was then grabbed up by the chaos of the post-war period. He finally finds his way back into life's harmonies." Bibliographer C.R. Owen states that German critic Hans Sochaczewer was one of the few to perceptively note that in *The Road Back* Remarque shows that the true hero is not the one who kills the enemy but the one who "simply manages to survive and who undauntedly retains his 'will to live.'"

The third book in the trilogy, *Three Comrades*, was not completed until 1937. It is the story of three friends, veterans of World War I, and the woman (modeled on Jutta) who becomes their comrade, their mutual romantic interest, and the lover of one. The men are struggling to reintegrate into normal society through their automobile mechanic business. Ultimately, the reader realizes that the only things of value to survive in these characters' lives are comradeship and love. *The Road Back* and *Three Comrades* also became best-sellers—though neither did as well as *All Quiet*. All were made into successful movies.

In 1937 Remarque got involved in a convoluted relationship with actress Marlene Dietrich, a fellow German expatriate. Biographer Julie Gilbert wonders whether this and Remarque's many other tortuous and obsessive relationships were related to the somewhat distant though loving relationship he had with his mother. Just as he could not quite get the attention and love he craved from his mother, so he seemed to seek out in his adult relationships women who were complex, demanding, self-centered, and mercurial—characteristics that might be applied to Remarque as well. Dietrich and Remarque carried on their ten-year affair, during which neither was monogamous (Gilbert points out that Remarque's pattern was to be involved in one deeply meaningful relationship and several casual dalliances at the same time), under the nose of Dietrich's husband and daughter, with whom they often traveled.

In January 1938, despite his new and passionate liaison with Dietrich, Remarque remarried Jutta. Her German passport was being revoked, and unless she was married to a Swiss resident, she would have to return to Germany. Remarque did not want to abandon her.

It was Dietrich who first caused Remarque to travel to the United States. Because of strained German and Swiss relations, German refugees like Remarque were being treated less than royally. Remarque was working well on a novel, but he missed Dietrich. In March 1939 he sailed to New York, traveling on a Panamanian passport because his German citizenship had been revoked. He then took a train to Hollywood. A few weeks later Remarque, Dietrich, her family, and another friend, traveled back to Europe to holiday in various places, ending up on the Riviera, a favorite vacation spot of celebrities. After a few months, Dietrich had to return to the United States for a film; the others remained until August, when, some reports say, Ambassador Joseph Kennedy (father of the future U.S. president), who was also vacationing there with his family, told Remarque and company that it was time to leave, that war was about to break out. Dietrich's husband, daughter, and Remarque fled on the *Queen Mary*, heading once again to New York. Jutta followed soon afterward but was detained because of passport problems. Remarque arranged for her to enter Mexico, where he once again rescued her.

AMERICA

Remarque settled into Hollywood for the next few years, where he became quite a celebrity. He was handsome and charming, wealthy and sophisticated, and he could identify any exotic liquor blindfolded, which proved a useful party trick. Unfortunately, he was also German at a time when the United States considered Germany a dangerous enemy. Remarque, like other "enemy aliens," was under a strict curfew from 6 P.M. to 8 A.M. and had to stay within five miles of his home. He wrote, "This curfew makes everything seem unrealistic, it's like waiting in a glass house: I read, move, don't work any longer, sleep, I'm without excitement or rebellion, just accepting the fact that we don't live any longer in Germany because we think democratic—and live in a democracy halfway incarcerated because we are Germans."

Nevertheless, he was able to work on several film scripts and, between parties, he continued working on his novels. *Flotsam* (1941) and *Arch of Triumph* (1945) both dealt with the theme of exile. The novels' characters are exiled from their home country. While traveling, they seek ways to survive financially (as noncitizens, it was extremely difficult to find legitimate work) and for new places to put roots, both geographically and emotionally. *Flotsam*'s title page contains the motto "To live without roots takes a stout heart." Ohio State University professor Charles Hoffmann suggests that Remarque should have added ". . . and continued good luck," as most of the characters in the novel run out of both.

Flotsam's sales and proceeds from the film version, *So Ends Our Night* (1941), were acceptable, but *Arch of Triumph* was an immediate hit. It is a complex melodrama featuring an exiled German physician reduced to performing illegal abortions, brothel health inspections, and other low-status work. He falls in love with a suicidal patient whom he restores to life but is ultimately unable to save. It was made into a less successful movie starring the great actors Charles Boyer, Ingrid Bergman, and Charles Laughton. In a 1968 interview, Remarque talked about how he crafted this novel that some consider one of his best:

> All I have done in writing was that I radically excised everything the reader would already know; I crossed off chapters, paragraphs, sentences, words, until I knew now I have to stop, or else it all falls apart. . . . I have always written scenes, I dramatized, all from one point, from one single person. Take Ravic [the doctor] in *Arch of Triumph:* If he disappears, so does the book. That gives it its tension. . . . People forget, in the face of its ease, how exactly the book had been crafted and why everything in it vibrates. . . . I write with my ears. I hear everything that I write; I select words according to their sounds . . . because I am musical.

Most of Remarque's novels featured heavy drinking—as did his life—but *Arch of Triumph* made such an impact that the brand of liquor mentioned throughout the novel, Calvados brandy, saw unprecedented sales for a time after the book's appearance.

By late 1942, Remarque had moved his American head-quarters to New York, a city he disliked when he first arrived but now found exciting, in part because his next serious love lived there. For the next several years he and Natasha Paley Wilson trysted at various European locations while Remarque worked on *Spark of Life*, a novel Charles W. Hoffmann describes as "the author's literary tribute to the suffering and determination of the victims of the concentration camps. . . . [His] theme is that death and horror will end and life will return." Simultaneously he was working on *A Time to Love and a Time to Die* (1954), a wartime love story set during the late years of the Third Reich.

CHANGE OF SCENE

In 1948, Remarque went back to his villa near Ascona, Switzer-land. He was having trouble writing *Spark of Life*, and he was feeling financial pressure as well as pressure from his pub-lisher. Biographer Julie Gilbert suggests that he had not been able to concentrate on his writing since the death of his sister, Elfriede, in 1943. She had been beheaded by the Nazis because of her "many months of unfettered, hateful, defeatist rumor-mongering." That she was the sister of the traitor Erich Maria Remarque was probably a factor in her sentence. Perhaps Re-marque believed that a change of scenery would once again in-spire his creative spark. Nevertheless, it took him nearly six more years to finish the book he had begun a decade before.

Remarque kept his New York apartment, dividing his time between Hollywood, New York, Ascona, and other European cities. But despite his American citizenship (acquired in 1947) and his declaration that "I am no longer German. Even when I dream, it is about America," his true geographic cen-ter gradually once again became Europe, where it remained until his death.

In 1950, Remarque recognized that he had some serious problems. His work was deteriorating, he was drinking more heavily than ever, and he was obsessively involved in a hope-less relationship with Natasha. He went into psychoanalysis to try to bring about some change in his life. He wrote in a diary,

> I always wanted to be more than I am, or wanted to appear more than that which I am. Always. . . . Perhaps I have found the source of my neurosis. . . . The two things in my life: to ap-pear to be more than I am, and the almost morbid dependency on love. . . . I am always acting the worldly man, the cavalier, the ladies' man—yet at the same time, I feel that I am a swindler and I'm no good as a writer, which will one day be-

come apparent. The cause: My childhood. For the first three years, until my brother Theo died, I am haunted by the words of my mother: that I was a very tender child, but had to be neglected, because it took three years for my brother to die. Thus: insecurity, loneliness, denial, feeling like I came in second and therefore was not lovable. . . .That's why I hang onto love and make renewed attempts to save what is lost.

PAULETTE

In April 1951, Remarque ran into the American actress Paulette Goddard, whom he had known in Hollywood. By May, they had started a relationship that would last until Remarque's death in 1970. Goddard was twelve years younger than Remarque and was filled with vitality and a zest for the good things in life. She started in show business while a young teenager and had been in several hit films. She was a cultured world traveler, and she loved jewels, furs, gifts of all sorts, and money, which she knew how to invest shrewdly. She had been married three times (very briefly when she was young; for several years to the great Charlie Chaplin, who some considered her Svengali and who made her film career take off; and to the actor Burgess Meredith).

Despite her broad experience in the world, Goddard maintained an aura of wholesomeness that was a welcome influence on Remarque. Early in their relationship, Remarque wrote of her: "Paulette wanders through the house, goes swimming, laughs, relaxes, happy, clear, goal-oriented, and apparently without any complexes. She feels good to me. She moves things into the right light." He noted later, "Everything is always the first time for her." Perhaps for the first time in a love affair, Remarque felt none of the sick obsessiveness he always experienced with the women he loved. Goddard was at ease and Remarque was, too. He also found that when she was away, he could work at home instead of restlessly drinking and socializing at restaurants and parties.

In 1952, Remarque and Goddard traveled to Germany, Remarque's first time back since his exile twenty years before. They visited Osnabrück, which had been all but destroyed during World War II. He saw his father for the last time, his surviving sister, Erna, and some old friends, including Hanns-Gerd Rabe. He felt as if he were in a dream; everything seemed foreign. He only returned to Germany one more time—briefly in 1954, after his father's death. Even when the city of Osnabrück wanted to give him a medal several years later, they had to come to him.

Remarque contributed to the screenplay adapted from his 1954 book *A Time to Love and a Time to Die,* and he even played a role in the movie. His first (and only) acting job received positive reviews.

Remarque's next novel, *The Black Obelisk* (1956), is generally described as the most autobiographical of his works—and all of them were autobiographical to some degree. He often drew characters from the people he had known; many of the books were clearly set in Osnabrück and other places he had lived. The protagonist of *The Black Obelisk* works as a tombstone salesman and moonlights as an organist at the local mental institution, as did Remarque as a young man. He falls in love with an impossible woman and loses her to death. Professor Charles W. Hoffmann considers it and *The Night in Lisbon* (1961) the best of Remarque's later works.

In late 1957, Remarque divorced Jutta for the second time (they had not lived together for several years); in May 1958, he and Paulette Goddard married. It was to be the last marriage for both of them, although she outlived him by twenty years. Remarque and Goddard had been spending half their year in Europe and half in New York. When Remarque's health began to fail in about 1960, Goddard continued to travel between the continents for several more years. She loved the excitement of New York, and she was continuing to do some film work. Additionally, according to biographer Julie Gilbert, Goddard's zest for life did not extend to illness; there are many hints that she did not enjoy being around Remarque in the little Swiss village as he grew weaker.

Despite his ill health, Remarque continued to write, producing a couple of plays and three more novels (*Heaven Has No Favorites*, 1961, a Hollywood story soundly panned by the critics; *The Night in Lisbon*, another novel of exile; and *Shadows in Paradise*, unfinished at the time of his death and, though clearly inferior to his other novels, published posthumously). He suffered a small stroke in 1962 and a series of heart attacks over the next few years.

Erich Maria Remarque died of a heart attack at Porto Ronco in 1970. His wife was at his side.

CHAPTER 1

The Voice of a Generation

READINGS ON
ALL QUIET ON THE
WESTERN FRONT

What *All Quiet on the Western Front* Means

Erich Maria Remarque

All Quiet on the Western Front became an immediate best-seller in nearly every country in which it was published. In only a few months, this war novel written by a German veteran had sold nearly a million copies in Germany (where it was both praised and reviled), nearly a half-million each in France, England, and the United States, and an impressive number in several other European countries. In constant demand by the public and the press, Erich Remarque, for the most part, avoided commenting publicly on his book. When Remarque's English publisher sent an advance copy of the novel to Sir Ian Hamilton, a British general, Hamilton wrote a letter to the publisher thanking him and telling him how true he felt the book was and how deeply it had touched him. The publisher forwarded the letter to Remarque, who responded with the letter below. The correspondence between the two men showed how two former enemies were able to find common ground in Remarque's description of the war experience of the common soldier.

June 1st, 1929

Dear Sir Ian Hamilton,

An extract from your letter to Mr. Huntington concerning my book, *All Quiet on the Western Front*, was very kindly sent on to me by the publishers, Messrs. Putnam. I intended to write to you about it at once, but was prevented from so doing during long weeks of illness which denied me the quiet hour I needed for my reply.

I cannot even now tell you which feeling was uppermost in me on receipt of your letter—whether that of personal

Excerpted from Erich Maria Remarque's letter to Sir Ian Hamilton, June 1, 1929, in *Life and Letters,* edited by Desmond MacCarthy, vol. 3, July 1929 to December 1929 (London: n.p.). Reprinted by permission of Pryor, Cashman, Sherman & Flynn, as agents for the Estate of Paulette Goddard Remarque.

pleasure, or of amazement and admiration at having been so clearly, so completely, so justly understood. Probably both were equally strong. You will be able to appreciate that I was entirely unaware what effect my work might produce outside Germany—whether I should have succeeded in making myself intelligible to all, or not.

A book on the war is readily exposed to criticism of a political character, but my work should not be so judged, for it was not political, neither pacifist nor militarist, in intention, but human simply. It presents the war as seen within the small compass of the frontline soldier, pieced together out of many separate situations, out of minutes and hours, out of struggle, fear, dirt, bravery, dire necessity, death and comradeship, into one whole mosaic, from which the word Patriotism is only *seemingly* absent, because the simple soldier never spoke of it. His patriotism lay in the *deed* (not in the *word*); it consisted simply in the fact of his presence at the front. For him that was enough. He cursed and swore at the war; but he fought on, and fought on even when already without hope. And of this there is, I believe, for those who can read, enough in my book.

But you, Sir Ian, have in a few words, exposed the very heart of my book, namely, the intention of presenting the fate of a generation of young men, who at the critical age, when they were just beginning to feel the pulse of life, were set face to face with death. I thank you for that most sincerely, and am delighted to hear these words from a man of high military rank. Your words are prized by me as those of a voice speaking clearly from England. In Germany it has never been forgotten how *fair* the English were, even in the midst of the battle, and so I am particularly pleased to find it confirmed in letters from English soldiers and English officers, that the background, the little things, but things so important for the individual soldier, were apparently similar on all the fronts.

UNDERSTANDING FOR A LOST GENERATION

I have not felt myself called upon to argue about the war. That must be reserved for the leaders, who alone know all that it is necessary to know. I merely wanted to awaken understanding for a generation that more than all others has found it difficult to make its way back from the four years of death, struggle and terror, to the peaceful fields of work and progress. Thousands upon thousands have even yet been unable to do it; countless letters from all countries have proved it to me. But all these letters say the same thing: 'We have been unable, because we did not know that our lethargy, our cynicism, our unrest, our hopelessness, our silence, our feeling of secession and exclusion arose from the fact that the regenerative power of our youth had been dissipated in the war. But now we will find the way, for you in your book have shown us the danger in which we stand, the danger of being destroyed by ourselves. But the recognition of a danger is the first step towards escape from it. We will now find our way back, for you have told us what it was that threatened us, and thereby it has become harmless.'

You see, Sir Ian, it is in this vein that my comrades write to me, and that proves that my book is only *seemingly* pessimistic. In reality, as it shows how much has been destroyed, it should serve as a call to them to rally for the peaceful battle of work and of life itself, the effort to achieve personality and culture. For the very reason that we had so early to learn to know death, we now want to shake off its paralysing spell—for we have seen it eye to eye and undisguised—we want to begin once again to believe in life. This will be the aim of my future work. He who has pointed out the danger, must also point out the road onward.

I have as yet never spoken my mind so fully; but your charming, appreciative letter compelled me to take up the pen in order to emphasize the two things in my book which, though not there in any very explicit way, are nevertheless there implicit—I mean, in the first place, the quiet heroism of the simple soldier, which lay precisely in the fact that he did not speak of it, that he did not perhaps so much as once realize it himself—speaking only of 'beans and bacon,' while all the time so much more lay behind that was other than this; and secondly, the fact that my book does not desire to preach resignation but rather than to be an S.O.S. call.

THE FUNDAMENTAL HUMAN WAR EXPERIENCE

You are right, Sir Ian, my book is not a 'perfect war book'. But such a war book, in the comprehensive sense, may not be written for yet another ten, perhaps even another hundred years. I restricted myself to the purely human aspect of war experience, the experience through which every man who went up to the front had to make his painful way: the fighting, the terror, the mastery, the power, the tenacity of the vital forces in the individual man faced with death and annihilation.

I like to regard that as the universal, fundamental experience; and I have aimed at describing without rhetoric and without political exploitation, this fundamental experience alone. And to this, I believe, may be attributed the success of my book, which in Germany has been read not merely in literary circles, but by those also who almost never take a book in their hands—by artisans, labourers, business people, mechanics, postmen, chauffeurs, apprentices, and so on; for many hundreds of letters all say: *'It is my own experience'.* The *outward* experience was, perhaps, in each case merely similar (though, as far as possible, I described only typical, standard situations, such as constantly recurred), but the decisive factor undoubtedly was that the book represented a part of the *inner* experience—Life confronting and fighting Death.

In conclusion, Sir Ian, allow me to thank you once again for your letter, and you may judge from the length of this how highly I valued it. I am happy to have met with such appreciative understanding.

Yours sincerely,
(*Signed*) Erich Maria Remarque

Why War Books Are Popular

Herbert Read

Sir Herbert Read was a British art historian, poet, and critic. He held academic posts at several universities, including Cambridge and Harvard. His book of poetry, *Naked Warriors* (1919), reflected his own experiences in World War I. In the following viewpoint, written as a review of a half-dozen war books, he discusses why, ten years after the end of the war, people had so much interest in war literature. He also discusses why there was a dearth of good material of this sort, and he names *All Quiet* as one of the best, a true work of art.

Ten years after the war, we find ourselves overtaken by a spate of war-books. There are several interesting questions connected with this phenomenon. Why, in the first place, have we had to wait ten years? For the explanation of that fact we must turn, not only to the soldiers themselves, but to the reading public. It must have been the experience of many men, when the war was over and they came back with minds seared with the things they had seen, to find a civilian public weary and indifferent, and positively unwilling to listen to them. The public was, indeed, suffering from a war-neurosis far worse than any the active soldier had contracted. There were many reasons why they should not want to listen to the soldier's tale. For example: (1) we are always jealous of the other man's experience when it might have been our own, even, and perhaps especially, if it was a tragic experience; (2) to encourage soldiers to speak and to reveal the enormity of the war would mean revealing the enormity of those who had instigated it and acquiesced in its continuance. The soldiers had one word before all others to express their views: Futility. How could any public, conscious of millions of dead and a nightmare of destruction, allow this word

Reprinted from Herbert Read, "Books of the Quarter," *Criterion*, April 1929.

to become current? For every man who did not fight in the war or against the war, fought for it. This applies in particular to the politicians and journalists, who had so debauched the public with their base and windy rhetoric as to make the bare truth treacherous. . . .

THE PUBLIC WANTS TO UNDERSTAND THE EXPERIENCE

Ten years have passed, and the public is asking for war books. It is cured of its shame-neurosis, and feels that it would like to know more about that great historic event through which it was fated to live. Or is the cause of this new interest the presence among us of a new generation that did not experience the war, but is curious to know what this great noise was that disturbed their infant slumbers? In any case, there appear to be a few soldiers ready to take advantage of the situation.

But can they? Potentially, yes. The number of those who took part in the war and who survive, and who had experiences of any value, is only a very small proportion of those who can claim war service. But even so, there must be tens of thousands, among the various combatant nations, with a story to tell. Among these there must be several hundreds technically capable of telling a story, if they had the will to do so. But for the majority there is no will, no way. Rudolf Binding tries to explain why. He has been writing bitterly and caustically about the wonderful stories related by war correspondents; he goes on to contrast the attitude of the true soldier:

'When I come to think of ourselves I notice many strangely silent folk amongst us. These are the men who have taken part in attacks and have lain under fire for hours and days—not like those who write about it in the newspapers. One meets a little dried-up Captain with a kindly nose, rather too large for him, and grey-blue eyes that seize and hold objects like those of a sparhawk. He sits in silence, seems to be cold, and sticks his hands together in his sleeves as in a muff. He is one of those who have been under fire in deadly earnest; and when he is warm at last and throws open his coat you may see that he wears the Iron Cross, First Class, on his breast, beneath his heart. If you are in luck and he happens to be in the mood you may hear something. How he lay right up forward with his company—nothing to the left, nothing to the right, nothing behind them. Yet they had orders to hold the trench. Then came the shells. Slowly searching they came, until one got the range; and there was no longer any trench in that spot, only a ragged crater. This was on the outer flank. Then came shell after shell, eating their way nearer and nearer. The men had to lie down; they had their orders that the trench must be held. Yet another ragged crater, not far from the first one. He sent back a message: 'Is no support coming up, to the right or the left, or behind me?' No support came; the reserves had been used up. But a fresh order came that the line was to be held at all costs. So they lay still.

'"Can't we retire, Herr Hauptmann?"' asked one of them who had never in his life made such a request before.

'"No."

'And so they lay there, waiting for the next shell; calculating that their trench was getting shorter and shorter, and that they would soon be without any cover at all; but there they lay—lay until the night came. There was not much left of the trench; but there was a chance to breathe. Then came another day—with the searching shells; then another night; and then—reliefs.

'The little Captain said nothing about the casualties. I could see that a picture inside his mind was keeping him from speaking. After a while he spoke again:

'"Heavy shells fly so slowly. One can hear them coming—a long way off. We had to keep lying down."

'That was all he had to say about the fire of heavy artillery. And once again I realized that experience makes one silent, or, at least, sparing of words.

'The history of this war will never be written. Those who can write it will remain silent. Those who write have not experienced it.'

Experience makes one silent. The history of this war will never be written. Those who could write it will remain silent. These words are worth repeating, and worth remembering.

ONLY THE POET CAN TRULY SHARE THE EXPERIENCE

That silence is only broken by exception. The exception is the poet. The poet is by definition a man who has the capacity to convert his spiritual experiences into words. The history of the war may never be written; but if it is written, it will be written by the poets who took part in it. That we may state as a general presupposition. But then their books will be of very different kinds. Broadly speaking, there are two possible categories. The first is the plain narrative—the journal or diary of day-to-day experiences. There is really no reason why this kind of narrative should not be written by any man with the habit of making notes, or with a memory as good as a notebook. But such men are the exception, and since the value and interest of a diary depends on the diarist possessing an eye for significant detail, we are reduced to our poets again, for this is another definition of the poet—a man with an eye for significant detail.

ARTISTIC FICTION

The second category is made up of those books in which the narrative has been arranged for imaginative or persuasive effect. No detail is false; the perspective is true. But the result is not a diary, but a work of art. This type of war-book is very rare, because normally the events are too violent to be easily subdued for the purposes of art. They are a hard kind of rock to hew into shape.

   To the first category belongs the interesting series of reprints published by Peter Davies (*Soldiers' Tales*, edited by Sir John Fortescue), and the fact that such volumes have to be dug up out of oblivion shows how little permanent impression they have made. The soldier's diary ends by interesting only the soldier, and perhaps a few historians. Why? *The Notebooks of Captain Coignet* is a good example of its kind: it is full of incident, of movement, of adventure; it throws vivid sidelights on great events. But it is all rather like an old newspaper—interesting if you have the ant-eating sort of mind, devouring little dead facts, but lifeless because formless. . . .

ALL QUIET SPEAKS FOR A GENERATION

The more important type of war-book is [the artistic work of fiction]. Herr Remarque . . . speaks for a generation rather than for an individual. His book is alone. It makes all other war books seem unnecessary. It achieves that which Binding says is impossible—the communication of experience. It is experience translated directly into terms of art and made universal. It deals with all the most terrible aspects of war, but we read it with tragic enjoyment. It is the greatest war-book that has yet appeared because it is the simplest, the starkest, and yet the most beautiful. Every significant phase of an infantryman's life at the Front is there, but not cast at the reader in the raw disorder of a diary, but subtly arranged to give the sense of reality without the sense of a limited point of view. It is not a pacifist book; it is not a humanitarian book; it is the truth, and to read it is to become filled with a passion for universal goodwill.

All Quiet Perfectly Transmits the Experience of War

Richard Church

Richard Church, himself a novelist and poet who had fought in World War I, believed that Erich Maria Remarque's remarkable little novel allowed the reader to truly understand the horrifying and brutalizing experience of those who fought in the Great War. In the following viewpoint, a review of *All Quiet* which he wrote for the London journal *The Spectator*, he points out how Remarque used intimate and telling details to depict the story of every soldier.

Surely everyone, again and again, has asked himself with misgiving and horror what is this conspiracy of silence maintained by the men who returned from the War? For it is true that, in spite of the many professional books written, no convincing revelation has been made of the heroism, the treachery, the foul intimacies, the brutality and coarseness, the gradual moral, social, and emotional decay, which made up, with a myriad other happier factors, the story of the soldier's life in the trenches. One timidly and somewhat shamefacedly asks questions of the individuals who were there, and the courteous and interested replies are always evasive and hopeless. It is as though the men despair of making one see the first elements of that world; as though they are trying to make one understand a race, a scenery, even a law of gravitation, peculiar to another planet, and so incapable of explanation in terrestrial terms to terrestrial senses.

THE TRUE EXPERIENCE

One, therefore, comes upon this book, and trembles. This is no literary trope; it is true. I read a few pages, and stopped. I returned, read on for a little, found myself living at last in that

Reproduced from Richard Church, "War," *The Spectator*, April 20, 1929, by permission of *The Spectator*, London.

world forbidden to the civilian, and again I had to stop, gropingly trying to orientate my mind, my nervous organism, to the overwhelming experience re-enacted by the genius of this German soldier. It is not an armchair experience, a vicarious life in the library. It is three-dimensional, nay, *four-dimensional* life, pulsing in one's arteries and loading one's brain with a weight of memories of things seen, heard, and suffered, so that one's life is no longer the same as it was; is older, more honest and disillusioned, stripped of false politeness and pruderies, and all the idle amenities of our normal social intercourse.

The author of this book—we have to call it a "book" for want of a more intense word—was twenty years old when he was seized by the German military monster. He went with six of his fellow-students. He came out alone. The others were dead or mad. These boys left a world of hope, enthusiasm, dawning scholarship and love, with tradition bursting like winter branches into the almond bloom of experience. Gradually the obtuse discipline of the army smoothed out the promise of personality and culture, effacing it like a picture swept by a tongue of fire. Civilized life, domestic reverie and books, these things became a broken memory that could not be reorganized, even when the soldier went on leave. He tried to do so. He shut himself up in his old bedroom, and took down his books:—

> Nothing stirs; listless and wretched, like a condemned man, I sit there and the past withdraws itself. And at the same time I fear to importune it too much, because I do not know what might happen then. I am a soldier, I must cling to that. Wearily I stand up and look out of the window. Then I take one of the books, intending to read, and turn over the leaves. But I put it away and take out another. There are passages in it that have been marked. I look, turn over the pages, take up fresh books. Already they are piled up beside me. Speedily more join the heap, papers, magazines, letters. I stand there dumb. As before a judge. Dejected. Words, Words, Words— they do not reach me. Slowly I place the books back in the shelves. Nevermore. Quietly, I go out of the room.

THE DEATH OF ALL THAT IS KNOWN

And not only the books. His old world was dead: barriers lay between him and his parents, his old associations. Even his mother dying of cancer and following him with pain-racked eyes as he moved about her bedroom on the last day of leave, even that was a remote, half-real sensation. "I ought never to

EXPERIENCES THAT BIND

A review of All Quiet on the Western Front *published in the* New Statesman *(May 25, 1929) points out that Remarque's novel managed to capture the universality of the experience of those who fought as ordinary soldiers in World War I.*

Most men who were engaged in active fighting during a long period of the war on the western front have felt that the human race is divided into two parts—those who shared in that experience and those who did not. The difference has nothing to do with a man's original character, still less with merit; it arises simply from the results of a unique and absolutely absorbing experience. It does not matter, from this point of view, on which side the combatants fought. We may infer from this book, as also from Mr. Blundeh, Mr. Mottra, Herr Arnold Zweig and many others, that an Englishman, a Frenchman, and a German who have lived that unsavoury life in the devastated zone have a stock of common knowledge which will bind them together for all time.

have come on leave," he said. The boys, while in the trenches, talked of these things, and tried to examine the change which was creeping over them like a paralysis.

Albert expresses it: "The War has ruined us for everything." He is right. We are not youth any longer. We are fleeing. We fly from ourselves. From our life. We were eighteen and had begun to love life and the world; and we had to shoot it to pieces. The first bomb, the first explosion, burst in our hearts. We are cut off from activity, from striving, from progress. We believe in such things no longer, we believe in the War.

And do you want to know, with an intimacy of horror that seems to stain one's very flesh, what the War is? You may learn here; of the degradation, of the treading of blood and filth and poison, of the unceasing din that shakes a soul out of life into death. You may see, for instance, the wounds inflicted by trench mortars:—

"He's been blown out of his clothes," mutters Tjaden. "It's funny," says Kat, "we have seen that a couple of times now. If a mortar gets you it blows you almost clean out of your clothes. It's the concussion that does it." I search round. And so it is. Here hang bits of uniform, and somewhere else is plastered a bloody mess that was once a human limb. Over there lies a body with nothing but a piece of the underpants on one leg and the collar of the tunic around its neck. Otherwise it is naked and the clothes are hanging up in the tree. Both arms are missing as though they had been pulled out. I discover one of them twenty yards off in a shrub. The dead man lies on his face. There, where the arm wounds are, the earth is black with blood. Underfoot the leaves are scratched up as though the man had been kicking. "That's no joke, Kat," say I.

There are other things of which you may learn; of the cruelty of lice, since they inflame not only a man's body but his soul; of the recrudescence of a barbaric worship of the obscene things of life, since "the soldier is on friendlier terms than other men with his stomach and intestines. Three-quarters of his vocabulary is derived from these regions, and they give an intimate flavour to expressions of his greatest joy as well as of his deepest indignation. It is impossible to express oneself in any other way so clearly and pithily. Our families and our teachers will be shocked when we go home, but here it is the universal language."

THE HELL NO NIGHTMARE CAN IMITATE

And there are other things to make one realize that in four years of this hell which no nightmare could imitate, the culture and intricately beautiful civilization built up since the beginning of human history, was torn off by these men as a frivolous appendage, and trampled angrily into the crimson-streaked mud of the trenches. But you may ask, "What, then, held these people together: what was that which kept them sane, and prompted them to such magnificent endurance, and to such ferocity of effort when occasion demanded?" And the answer is simply, "Comradeship." That is the soul of this book. It was the young soldier's one light. He had been too young to find anchorage in love, religion, or a profession. No memories of these things, no hope of return to them, were there to support him. Comradeship was his substitute for these forces, and by its strength he conquered death, and carried through to some sort of preservation.

What that preservation was, still remains for that war-shattered generation to discover. One may hope that it will be complete; that a new world of purpose and achievement may result from a gradual reintegration of the broken vitality; that the disease which no spiritual doctors can diagnose may slowly be dispelled by time and peace. The author is not so hopeful:—

I am young. I am twenty years old; yet I know nothing of life but despair, death, fear, and fatuous superficiality cast over an abyss of sorrow. I see how peoples are set against one another, and in silence, unknowingly, foolishly, obediently, innocently slay one another. I see that the keenest brains of the world invent weapons and words to make it yet more refined and enduring. And all men of my age, here and over there, throughout the whole world, see these things; all my generation is experiencing these things with me. What would our fathers do if we suddenly stood up and proffered our account? What do they expect of us if a time ever comes when the War is over? Through the years our business has been killing; it was our first calling in life. Our knowledge of life is limited to death. What will happen afterwards? And what shall come out of us?

A word must be said of the translation. It is a model of English prose; simple, dignified, and rising at times to a poetic power worthy of the Old Testament. It has been done by one of the men who lived and suffered in the trenches, one who fought against the fellow-artist whose book he has now so graciously introduced to the English-speaking world.

All Quiet Is an Immature Novel of Adolescent Self-Pity

William K. Pfeiler

All Quiet on the Western Front has been widely praised as an antiwar novel, but William K. Pfeiler argues that more realistically the novel represents spoiled youth's whining about the older generation. In the novel, Remarque depicts lively, healthy young men enslaved to the war god by their elders. It is thus their elders' fault not only that many of them die, but that they are deprived of the "normal" experiences of late adolescence and are unable to return to civilization. This picture gives them a perfect excuse for aimlessness and lack of achievement after the war. Pfeiler questions whether Paul Bäumer would have fared any better had he not been caught up in World War I. At the time he wrote the following selection, Pfeiler taught at the University of Nebraska.

Life at the front is hard. It is hard for any man, even the big, hulking farmhands who have not a soft bone in their bodies, even on the city boys who are always ready for a scrap. But how much harder for the men who have learned to feel things deeply!

There is in Western culture a whole school of training which—unconsciously or not—centers upon sensibility. The artists and musicians and poets must feel deeply all things, life itself. For how can they create works of art without a mental acuteness of sensation? And if their whole training is to develop delicacy of mind and feeling, they certainly cannot have had a more inept preparation for life at the front!

Some of the best of war novels present the reaction of men of feeling to the war. They do not agree with one another, and

From *War and the German Mind*, by William K. Pfeiler. Copyright © 1941, Columbia University Press. Reprinted with the permission of the publisher.

naturally, for individual response is the essence of their training. Some are disappointing, and some reward the reader. . . .

Neither in length, scope, nor importance can the work of Erich Maria Remarque, whose novel *Im Westen nichts Neues* [*All Quiet on the Western Front*] (1928), became a world sensation, be compared to the epic achievement of [Arnold] Zweig. Its success will perhaps never be satisfactorily explained, but one fact seems certain: it cannot be due exclusively to extraordinary merit.

ARTISTIC BUT SIMPLISTIC

Remarque is an artist. By his impressionistic talent he knows how to draw characters and situations that engage attention and arouse deepest sympathy. His language is versatile and concise; his narrative is rich in contrast of situations and reflections, and his composition is done with a brilliant stage technique. Lyric and idyllic scenes alternate with the most lurid and coarsest sort of realism. The intricate problems of life and of the War are cleverly reduced to such plain propositions that even the poorest in spirit can grasp them. Just at the most favorable psychological moment, when Zweig had broken the ice and the universal antiwar sentiment had reached its very climax, Remarque's story gave expression to the cry "No More War!"

But what are the facts and ideas of this book which claimed to tell of the fate of a whole generation?

A number of adolescents, college students, have been induced by their teacher to volunteer for war service. They and a few older men form a group somewhere at the Western Front. Their fate is the subject of the story, which was to be "neither an accusation nor a confession" but an attempt to give a report of "a generation that was destroyed by war, even though it might have escaped its shells." These pretensions of the author must be refuted. Ample evidence shows that the heroes of Remarque are not representative of a whole generation, but only of a certain type. This is not to criticize Remarque for military and other inconsistencies, but it is significant that in a book which claims to be a report of the front by a front soldier, of 288 pages of text only about 80 pages deal with situations at or right behind the front, and even they are heavily interspersed with reflections. Furthermore, it may be characteristic that the actual life at the front is described in general terms without ever a definite location given, while scenes behind the front, at hospitals, at home, in the barracks, etc., are given in a more clearly outlined realism. The implication is obvious; it leaves little doubt that many of his situations are fictitious.

UNFAIR INDICTMENT OF THE OLDER GENERATION

What is more, the ethical character of the book provokes critical reflection. Through sordid detail and the description of gruesome and inhuman happenings, through reflection and innuendo, the condemnation of war amounts in the last analysis to a sweeping indictment of the older generation. It is as simple as that, and it would not evoke any criticism on our part, the guilt of the elders being a genuine problem, were it not for the superficial way in which Remarque goes about his task. Their teachers get the blame for the boys' being in a war which is of use "only to the Kaiser and the generals." With adolescent swagger, they call all culture "nonsense" [*Quatsch*] because they have to be out at the front, and when they have a chance they will pay their torturers back. For example, we find the hero on leave at home and looking at his books, among them all of the classical writers. He says: "I have read them with honest zeal, but most of them did not quite appeal to me; so much the more did I appreciate the other books, the more modern ones." This statement provides a good insight into the mind of the hero and his lack of appreciation for the values of the classical tradition. Again Lieutenant Mittelstedt "gets even" with his former teacher, now a drafted private. This particular scene, told with the malicious glee of an adolescent, is typical of the immature and sophomoric attitude of the heroes. So is the ever-recurring swagger and boastfulness of the young men who pose as old warriors well versed in all the tricks of warfare, though there is not one description of a feat actually executed, such as we find so abundantly and realistically in many other war books.

Individual incidents are given typical significance, less by an abstract process than by the exclusiveness with which they are presented. Thus the reader gets the impression that all officers are brutes; all teachers are cowardly shirkers who let others do the bloody and dangerous job of fighting for Germany's glory while they stay safely at home; and all doctors are inhuman monsters. Against this world of brutality are set off in shining lights the simple but genuine virtues of the common soldiers. They are all good fellows, and it arouses our sympathy to see them fall prey to power-drunk, sadistic superiors.

IMMATURE AND BIASED

Immaturity and partiality by omission detract from the ethical import of this work which must be admitted to have force and human appeal. That the writer projects his 1927 mentality into the life of young World War soldiers is perhaps not so great a defect as is his wilfully narrowed outlook. *Im Westen nichts Neues* is scarcely a serious ethical document. Rather it is symptomatic of an age that saw the final revelation of the war in the adolescent self-pity, resentment, and sentimentality the novel embodies. Really it is the story of an egocentric, immature youngster of whom one may well wonder how he would have developed without the war. There is, indeed, plenty of authority for holding that the war helped many to find themselves and prove their mettle, and that it also exposed the brittle human substance that might have been broken by life anyway, without ever having been exposed to the destructive shells of war. It goes without saying that this observation—contradicting point-blank Remarque's claim to speak for a whole generation—implies neither that the war did not destroy the best of human values, nor that war was justifiable because it developed character.

All Quiet Reflects the Postwar Mind

Modris Eksteins

All Quiet on the Western Front is often praised for the way it faithfully captures not only the physical experience of war, but the psychological bent of the young soldiers who were caught up in its futile and alienating brutality. Modris Eksteins, professor of history at the University of Toronto, Canada, argues in the following viewpoint that it is more accurate to say that Remarque captured the *post*war mind. After all, when Remarque wrote the novel, the war had been over for ten years. Remarque and other writers of his generation were finally able to come to terms with the trauma the war had caused them, and Remarque, like a number of other writers, wrote the novel during this post-trauma time, not during the war. Consequently, it reflects postwar values, including the belief that World War I contributed immensely to the rootlessness of many of the people who survived it. Modris Eksteins has written extensively about Germany's Weimar Republic and on war and its impact on civilization.

The simplicity and power of the theme—war as a demeaning and wholly destructive, indeed nihilistic, force—are made starkly effective by a style that is basic, even brutal. Brief scenes and short crisp sentences, in the first person and in the present tense, create an inescapable and gripping immediacy. There is no delicacy. The language is frequently rough, the images often gruesome. The novel has a consistency of style and purpose that Remarque's earlier work had lacked and that little of his subsequent work would achieve.

Despite Remarque's introductory comment and his reiteration of the point in later statements, very few contemporary reviewers noted, and later critics have generally ignored, that *All Quiet* was not a book about the events of the war—it was not a memoir, much less a diary—but an angry declaration about the effects of the war on the young generation that lived through it. Scenes, incidents, and images were chosen to illustrate how the war had destroyed the ties, psychological, moral, and real, between the generation at the front and society at home. "If we go back," says Paul, "we will be weary, broken, burnt out, rootless, and without hope. We will not be able to find our way any more." The war, Remarque was asserting in 1928, had shattered the possibility of pursuing what society would consider a normal existence.

THE POSTWAR MIND

Hence, *All Quiet* is more a comment on the postwar mind, on the postwar view of the war, than an attempt to reconstruct the reality of the trench experience. In fact that reality is distorted, as many critics insisted—though with little effect on the initial acclaim for the novel. Remarque's critics said that at the very least he misrepresented the physical reality of the war: a man with his legs or his head blown off could not continue to run, they protested vehemently, referring to two of the images Remarque had used. But far more serious than such shoddiness, they claimed, was his lack of understanding of the moral aspects of soldiers' behavior. Soldiers were not robots, devoid of a sense of purpose. They were sustained by a broad spectrum of firmly established values.

Although his publisher did not like such admissions, because they undermined the credibility of the novel, Remarque was prepared to say that his book was primarily about the postwar generation. In an exchange in 1929 with General Sir Ian Hamilton, the British commander at Gallipoli in 1915 and now head of the British Legion, Remarque expressed his "amazement" and "admiration" that Hamilton for one had understood his intentions in writing *All Quiet*:

I merely wanted to awaken understanding for a generation that more than all others has found it difficult to make its way back from four years of death, struggle, and terror, to the peaceful fields of work and progress.

It was in part the misinterpretation of his purpose that led Remarque to write a sequel to *All Quiet. Der Weg zurück* (*The Road Back*), a novel published in 1931, explicitly argued the case of the "lost generation."

FACE TO FACE WITH DEATH

In an interview with Axel Eggebracht for Die Literuische Welt, a German periodical, Erich Maria Remarque commented on the subject matter of his wildly successful novel. The following excerpt was translated for the Boston Transcript *and reprinted in an article in the October 12, 1929,* Literary Digest.

Our generation has grown up in a different way from all others before and afterward. Their one great and most important experience was the war. No matter whether they approved or rejected it; whether they understood it from a nationalistic, pacifistic, adventurous, religious, or stoic point of view. They saw blood, horror, annihilation, struggle, and death. That was the general human experience of all. And I have confined myself intentionally to this one experience. The war is presupposed as a fact sufficiently well known. The few reflections which are to be found in the book occupy themselves with this purely human experience of the war. I avoided taking sides from every political, social, religious or other point of view. I consider myself just as little competent to do this as to write a history of the war. I have spoken only of the terror, of the horror, of the desperate, often brutal impulses of self-preservation, of the tenacious hold on life, face to face with death and annihilation.

All Quiet can be seen not as an explanation but as a symptom of the confusion and disorientation of the postwar world, particularly of the generation that reached maturity during the war. The novel was an emotional condemnation, an assertion of instinct, a *cri d'angoisse* [a cry of anguish] from a malcontent, a man who could not find his niche in society. That the war contributed enormously to the shiftlessness of much of the postwar generation is undeniable; that the war was the root cause of this social derangement is at least debatable; but Remarque never took part in the debate directly. For Remarque the war had become a vehicle of escape. Remarque and his book were, to borrow from Karl Kraus, symptoms of the disease they claimed to diagnose.

Notwithstanding Remarque's opening declaration of impartiality—that his book was "neither an accusation nor a confession"—it was in fact both. And it was more. It was a confession of personal despair, but it was also an indignant denunciation of an insensate social and political order, inevitably of that order which had produced the horror and destruction of the war but particularly of the one that could not settle the war and deal with the aspirations of veterans. Through characters identifiable with the state—the schoolmaster with his unalterable fantasies about patriotism and valor, the former postman who functions like an unfeeling robot in his new role as drill sergeant, the hospital orderlies and doctors who deal not with human suffering, only bodies—Remarque accused. He accused a mechanistic civilization of destroying humane values, of negating charity, love, humor, beauty, and individuality. Yet Remarque offered no alternatives. The characters of his *generazione bruciata*—the Italian notion of a "burned generation" is apt—do not act; they are merely victims. Of all the war books of the late twenties—the novels of Arnold Zweig, Renn, R.H. Mottram, H.M. Tomlinson, Richard Aldington, Hemingway, and the memoirs of Graves, Blunden, Sassoon, to name but a few of the more important works—Remarque's made its point, that his was a truly lost generation, most directly and emotionally, even stridently, and this directness and passion lay at the heart of its popular appeal.

CHAPTER 2

A Work of Art

All Quiet's Emotional Realism Is Its Strength

Frank Ernest Hill

When *All Quiet on the Western Front* appeared in the United States, critics and readers greeted it enthusiastically. In fact, it was said to have sold more copies than any book except the Bible. Why did it receive such a reception? Frank Ernest Hill, a reviewer for the New York *Herald Tribune*'s Sunday book section, said it was because the book made the reader vicariously experience what the soldiers in the trenches had experienced. Hill notes that other books written about the war were richer in detail, but none of them had the same impact on the reader that *All Quiet* did.

It is a terrible thing that a great book should fall into an indifferent world and a sad thing that even a good one should go neglected. And since "All Quiet on the Western Front" is undoubtedly a good book and possibly a great one, the volleys of acclaim by publisher and critics which accompany it may deserve our patience if not our gratitude. Yet in the making of an independent appraisal they are confusing. Let us forget for the moment that "this is the greatest book about the war that I have yet seen," and that the translation has "a poetic power worthy of the Old Testament," and discover what, in a more literal sense, the volume is.

Erich Maria Remarque was a German soldier during the World War and has written a record of life in the trenches. To the extent at least that the hero dies in October, 1918, and Herr Remarque still lives to write publicity and draw royalties, the book is fiction. Yet it is obviously founded on indelible fact and might be an authentic autobiographical account.

We come upon the hero and his companions when they are already a part of the war machine. There are Katczinsky and Müller, Kropp and Behm, Tjaden, Westhus, Detering

Reprinted from Frank Ernest Hill, "Destroyed by the War," *New York Herald Tribune*, Books section, June 2, 1929.

and Paul Bäumer, who tells the story. They are young men most of them; in fact, it was their schoolmaster, Kantorek, who persuaded some of them to enlist. We see in casual flashbacks their former boyish enthusiasm and how this was taken out of them by Corporal Himmelstoss, an absurd little martinet who made discipline abominable and war by contrast a thing that could be borne. And as the terse story marches forward we encounter the things that other war books have made known to us: the trench mud, the lice, the ineradicable rats, the tension, noise, fear, pain, hunger, horror. One by one the group melts away. When Bäumer sinks into the darkness that takes so many soldiers he is the last.

On this long pilgrimage, so often ghastly and ferocious, there is more than the routine of the trenches. There are glimpses of the land back of the lines, with its millions of illustrious madmen, fools and knaves. There are hospital scenes. There is a prison camp. There is battle in the "open." There is the almost pitifully childish thread of comradeship, touching, pathetic, human, which runs from first to last. There is the brief joviality of geese stolen and secretly roasted, of Himmelstoss and Kantorek under arms, "getting theirs." Perhaps most important there is the inner drama—the fever that rises and falls in the souls of the fighters as the war goes on. To this, indeed, the whole story is shaped—its sharply etched descriptions of suffering, endurance, grim humor and climactic event.

Much of this bears resemblance to older books; in a sense there is little of it which [nineteenth-century French novelist Henri] Barbusse did not see and feel. Barbusse gives a similar detail and in many ways more richly; his canvas is closer to [French novelist Victor] Hugo's and Remarque's to something between [the novelists Guy de] Maupassant's and [Gustave] Flaubert's. As to writing, you will find more color and music, and, sentence by sentence, art, in Edmund Blunden's "Undertones of War." And I suspect that to compare the excellent English prose of Mr. Wheen's translation to the best of the Old Testament may be close to piffle.

A WORK OF ART

Yet "All Quiet on the Western Front" will give any sensitive reader a terrific impact. It is a book that strikes a succession of hard, inescapable blows. In this sense it is a work of art. For only because of its economy of design, its compactness of episode and its trenchancy of utterance has it managed to fuse the almost unmanageable minutiae of war material into a narrative that has the lean savagery of an Ibsen tragedy. It pays in loss of color and sense of greatness for this concentration of utterance, yet the price is perhaps not too big. It is a pity, incidentally, that the title, which in the original pointed up the whole story, is blurred out of its meaning in translation. "Im Westen Nicht Neues" is a phrase taken from the final paragraph. The hero has died and the official report reads literally: "In the west nothing new." Obviously this applies to the book itself; the war wiped out the man who wrote it and never counted the loss. Mr. Wheen loses this final tremendous irony, though it is probably one of the inevitable losses of any translation.

One could quote much and poignantly from this record. There are passages of vulgar humor, Germanic yet universal in character. There are dying men with features "uncertain and faint, like a photographic plate on which two pictures have been taken." There are the men caught in a barrage who happen to be in a cemetery and find later that they have been using disinterred coffins and corpses for shields. They are glad to get a coffin board for a splint. There is the incredible battle:

> No one would believe that in this howling waste there could still be men; but steel helmets now appear on all sides of the trench, and fifty yards from us a machine gun is already in position and barking.

The psychology of the fighter, emerging from his dugout after a three-day bombardment, has a new grim twist here:

> We have already become wild beasts. We do not fight; we defend ourselves against annihilation. It is not against men that we fling our bombs. What do we know of men in this moment, when Death with hands and helmets is hunting us down? Now, for the first time in three days, we can see his face; now, for the first time in three days, we can oppose him; we feel a mad anger. No longer do we lie helpless, waiting on the scaffold; we can destroy and kill, to save ourselves, to save ourselves and be revenged.

Like a sad night wind in contrast to this spitting volcano of utterance comes the description of the Russian prisoners:

> In the darkness one sees their forms like sick storks, like great birds. They come close to the wire fence and lean their faces against it; their fingers hook round the mesh. Often many stand side by side and breathe the wind that comes down from the moors and the forest. . . . A word of command has made these silent figures our enemies; a word of com-

mand might transform them into our friends. At some table a document is signed by some persons whom none of us knows, and then for years together that very crime on which formerly the world's condemnation and severest penalty fell becomes our highest aim. But who can draw such a distinction when he looks at these men with their childlike faces and apostles' beards! Any non-commissioned officer is more of an enemy to a recruit, any schoolmaster to a pupil, than they are to us. And yet we would shoot at them again and they at us if they were free.

The most remarkable incident of the book is the description of Bäumer's murder of the printer, Gérard Duval. In the eighteen pages which comprise this incident a great deal is told about war. The "murder" is almost inevitable, certainly natural, and therefore the more appalling. But the details deserve to be held for those who read books and not reviews.

Remarque says in a few sentences of foreword that he will "try to tell of a generation of men who, even though they have escaped its shells, were destroyed by war." This task is well performed. Never obtruding his feelings, he reveals them naturally and convincingly as they grow. These young men:

> What do they expect of us if a time ever comes when the war is over? Through the years our business has been killing—it was our first calling in life. Our knowledge of life is limited to death.

And again:

> Now if we go back we will be weary, broken, burnt out, rootless and without hope. . . . The generation that grew up before us, though it has passed these years with us here, already had a home and a calling; now it will return to its old occupations, and the war will be forgotten—and the generation that has grown up after us will push us aside. We will be superfluous even to ourselves, we will grow older, a few will adapt themselves, some others will merely submit, and most of us will be bewildered—the years will pass by, and in the end we shall fall into ruin.

This philosophy, rounding out the compact record, is in its permeative quality German. So, perhaps, is the thorough devotion to duty which seems to leave the soldiers incurious as to their enemies, except in prison camps. Yet the book is surprisingly un-national; it might almost have been written by a Frenchman or an American, or an English common soldier of intelligence—it lacks the overtones of a book by an Englishman with a public school education. It remains a gaunt, dynamic thing, lacking, I feel, something important in literary texture, speaking with remarkable directness of life-in-death.

All Quiet Is an Artfully Constructed Novel

Brian A. Rowley

The literary merit of *All Quiet on the Western Front* has been debated by critics ever since it was first published. Its extreme popularity was enough to convince some critics that it had little literary value; the fact that it appealed to the popular mind meant that the author clearly had analyzed what sold best and structured his novel accordingly. Other critics, however, point out that rather than pandering to public taste, Remarque has skillfully interwoven story, language, style, and structure to create a world readers can immerse themselves in.

Brian A. Rowley thinks the novel has literary merit. At the time he wrote the following viewpoint, Rowley was professor of European literature at the University of East Anglia in England. German literature of the late nineteenth century was one of his areas of specialty. Here, he analyzes Remarque's literary technique: his use of sensual detail to show the importance of the fantasy of creature comforts to the psychological survival of soldiers; his use of nature as a backdrop and integral symbol in the novel; his language and syntax; his choice of the first-person narrator; and his novel's structure.

Remarque's success was due [to its timing, but] also to the book's intrinsic qualities.* Some of these, we may feel, are journalistic rather than strictly literary. The particular blend of suffering, sensuality and sentiment suggests that Remarque

---

*The two sensitive interpretations of *Im Westen* which have appeared in the last decade are both presented as comparisons with Anglo-Saxon works: with *A Farewell to Arms*, in Helmut Liedloff 'Two War Novels: A critical comparison', *Rev. litt. comp.* 42 (1968) pp. 390–406; and with *Her Privates We*, in Holger M. Klein, 'Dazwischen Niemandsland: *Im Westen nichts Neues* und *Her Privates We*', in *Grossbritannien und Deutschland . . . Festschrift für John W.P. Bourke*, ed. Ortwin Kuhn (München: Wilhelm Goldmann Verlag, 1974) pp. 487–512.

Reprinted from Brian A. Rowley, "Journalism into Fiction: *Im Westen nichts Neues*," in *The First World War in Fiction: A Collection of Critical Essays*, edited by Holger Klein (London: Macmillan, 1976), by permission of the author.

had gauged public taste. The horror and degradation of war is represented, but it is shown with irony, wit, and even humour. To a large extent, this is made possible by the choice of a group of characters who are close to the reader. And this again depends upon Remarque's command of a clear but lively, indeed pungent style. . . .

Let us look at some of these aspects more closely. The sensuality, for example. 'We have lost our sense of other connections, because they are artificial. Only the facts are real and important to us'. And sensual comforts are facts, just as much as war's horrors. Remarque loses no time in foregrounding these comforts in Chapter I. The novel starts with food ('a belly full of haricot beans and stewed beef'); with tobacco ('for every man, ten cigars, twenty cigarettes and two sticks of chewing tobacco, that can't be bad'); and with sleep ('war wouldn't be so bad, if only we had more sleep'). But the soldier's idea of comfort doesn't stop here: the 'decencies' of ordinary society have been left behind, and so, when the novel opens, Remarque's heroes spend two hours sitting in the sunshine on little portable thunder-boxes, talking and playing skat; and Paul comments: 'Here in the open air this business is a real pleasure to us . . . To the soldier, his belly and his digestion are more familiar than they are to anyone else. Three-quarters of his vocabulary is taken from that area . . .'. Scatological terms certainly do appear in the characters' vocabulary—though less often than they would have done in real life. Again, in Chapter III the nakedness of Himmelstoss before his whipping is made explicit.

Unlike defecation, copulation is only lightly suggested in the early chapters. Paul's fellow-soldier Leer has 'a beard and a great liking for girls from the officers' brothels; he swears they are required by army orders to wear silk shifts and, for customers of the rank of captain and above, to take a bath beforehand'. In Chapter V, one of the answers to the question, What would you do if the war ended today?—that by Haie Westhus—revolves around women. But the main sex-scene is kept for Chapter VII when—ironically after Haie Westhus's fatal back-wound has been reported—Leer, Kropp and Paul swim naked across a canal at night to visit the three Frenchwomen they have propositioned. After the food they have brought has been eaten, the six of them make love:

> There are rooms close by . . . How different all this is from
> things in the other ranks' brothels, which we're allowed to
> visit and where there are long queues. I don't want to think

of them; but unbidden they pass through my mind, and I take
fright, for perhaps one can never ever forget such things.

But then I feel the lips of the slim, dark girl, and I push myself towards them; I close my eyes, as if to shut it all out—war
and horror and vulgarity—to wake up young and happy . . . And
I press myself all the more deeply into the arms that enfold
me; perhaps a miracle will occur.

The sexuality is unmistakable; but so is the restraint.

FOCUS ON CREATURE COMFORTS VITAL TO SOLDIERS' MENTAL SURVIVAL

The fact that *All Quiet* was read for its indecencies was
recognised from the start. 'Many read it mainly for its im-
proprieties', writes an early [German] commentator; and the
impact made by the latrine-scene in Chapter I and the sex-
scene in Chapter VII may be gauged from the emphasis on
them in the parody *All Quiet at the Gates of Troy*. This was
certainly a reason for the novel's success. Yet Remarque
never lets indecency become obscene, still less pornographic. More important, he is able to show, because of the
point of view of his narrative, that an emphasis on creature
comforts is part of the soldier's psychology; less trivially realistic, that it is part of his defence against the otherwise un-
bearable brutality of war. This is illustrated, in the farcical
mode, by the goose-roasting sequence in Chapter V after the
horrors of the wire-laying fatigue in IV; and in the lyrical
mode, by the love-scene in Chapter VII after the battle-scene
of VI. And finally—as Paul's love-scene with his brunette
suggests—it is a mode of experience through which the soldier's contact with the deepest springs of life, threatened as
it is by war, can be renewed. All these points are made in
Paul's meditation earlier in VII, which concludes:

But our comrades are dead, we cannot help them, they are at
rest—who knows what faces us? what we want is to lie down
and sleep or eat as much as we can get into our bellies, and
drink and smoke, so that the hours are not empty. Life is short.

Sensuality in the novel functions on many levels.

NATURE'S ROLE

The same is true of external nature. When the three walk
back along the river-bank after their love-scene:

The night air cools our hot bodies. The poplars tower up into the
darkness and rustle. The moon is in the sky and in the water of
the canal. We do not run, we walk side by side taking long strides.

The poplars here are counter-images to war; but they are also priapic and, thereby, metaphysical, even religious symbols. A simpler contrast is produced by the scene after the soldiers leave their trucks, in the wire-laying episode of Chapter IV:

> Mist and gun-smoke lie chest-high over the fields. The moon shines on them. On the road, troops are passing. The steel helmets give back dull gleams in the moonlight. Heads and rifles stand out above the white mist; nodding heads, swaying rifle-barrels.

> Nearer the front the mist ends. The heads become figures here; coats, trousers and boots emerge from the mists as if from a pool of milk.

Mist and moonlight make a backcloth for the devastation that is to follow. One of the most reverberant examples of this technique of juxtaposition is provided by the passage when Paul leaves the hospital after Kemmerich's death at the end of Chapter II:

> Outside the door I feel the darkness and the wind as a kind of salvation. I breathe as deeply as possible, and feel the air warm and soft, as never before, against my face. Thoughts of girls, of meadows in flower, of white clouds flash suddenly through my head. . . . The earth is permeated by forces which flow into me through the soles of my feet. The night crackles electrically, the front thunders dully like a concert of drums. My limbs move supplely, I feel my joints are strong, I pant and blow. The night lives, I live. I feel a hunger, greater than that of the belly alone.

Liedloff suggests that the motif of the 'butterfly' provides a particular instance of such juxtaposition.

Nature, too, then, restores the lost contact with life. The intimate connections between war and nature are reinforced by Remarque's use, from time to time, of a grammatical device—a kind of zeugma which links, without overt comment, experiences from the two spheres:

> It smells of tar, summer, and sweaty feet.

> Then, once again, there are only the rockets, the singing of the shells, and the stars . . .

WAR'S BRUTAL REALITY

On the success of Remarque's rendering of the brutal reality of war there has been, from the beginning, more agreement than on most other issues. Some details, certainly, were challenged: notably the screaming of the wounded horses, in Chapter IV. But other critics were quick to point out literary

analogues in [American novelist James] Fenimore Cooper—
incidentally one of the authors Remarque recalls admiring
in his teens—in [the novelists] Liliencron, and in Zola;
whilst a veterinary surgeon confirmed that horses do indeed
scream when in pain. It was also, more widely, argued that
war is not always so brutal and so ignominious as this novel
depicts it; but that is to miss the point that trench warfare in
Flanders in 1914–18 is not war in general, but a particulari-
sation of the brutalising tendencies inherent in all warfare to
a point of no return. And this sort of warfare *is* captured by
Remarque's sober realism, more successfully than ever before; as Friedrich Fuchs wrote [in the German journal
Hochland] when the novel's sales reached a million: 'I can
only explain it like this: you can read here, for the first time,
what it was really like out there.' This success, which lies at
the heart of Remarque's achievement, was summarised by
the Expressionist dramatist Ernst Toller, in a review that became famous:

> No modern writer has more magnificently evoked a battle, a
> gas-attack, hand-to-hand fighting, a visit home on leave; I
> shall never forget the hail of fire over the graveyard, or the dy-
> ing of the helpless wounded horses . . .

> This is how German soldiers lived in the trenches, and
> French ones, and British ones.

How does Remarque manage to evoke the reality of battle?
Let us look at a passage from the graveyard section (in IV)
which Toller praises:

> The fields are flat, the wood is too far and too dangerous;
> there is no other cover but the graveyard and the mounds. In
> the dark we stumble in, each man is at once glued to the back
> of a mound as if spat there.

> Not a moment too soon. The darkness becomes insane. It
> heaves and rages. Blacker darknesses than the night, hugely
> bulging, rush towards us, over us. The flames from the ex-
> plosions flicker across the graveyard.

> Nowhere is there an escape. In the flash of the shells I risk a
> look at the fields. They are a sea in turmoil; the jets of flame
> from the shells jump up like fountains. It is impossible for
> anyone to get across there alive.

> The wood disappears, it is pounded, torn, shredded out of ex-
> istence. We will have to stay here in the graveyard.

> In front of us the earth bursts. It rains clods. I feel a jolt. My
> sleeve is torn by a splinter. I clench my fist. No pain. But that
> doesn't reassure me, wounds never hurt until later. I run my
> hand over the arm. It is scratched, but whole.

No Exaggeration

For the most part, a blow-by-blow account of successive events. Only at a few points—'The darkness becomes insane'; 'a sea of turmoil'—does the language heighten and interpret. For the rest, no understatement certainly; but no exaggeration either. Even the description of the annihilation of the little wood—'it is pounded, torn, shredded out of existence'—convinces us that its rhetorical accumulation is no more than sober truth. This consistent and determined factuality is the key to Remarque's total success in depicting trench warfare.

In a 1929 interview . . . Remarque claimed not to have read the war novels of either Barbusse or Unruh; and his descriptions do not give the impression of deriving from literary models. It is rather that his experience as a journalist has taught him how to select facts and convey them in a style that heightens, rather than blurs, their impact; and that this journalistic skill is here put to literary use.

Remarque's Syntax

To say this, however, is to remind ourselves that truth is a matter of style as much as of content. The style of *All Quiet* has been more praised than analysed. A striking feature of the syntax is the prevalence of simple—one-verb—sentences, and of compound ones without coordinating conjunctions, or at most with 'and'. Complex sentences with their subordinating conjunctions and, in German in particular, their less immediately penetrable thought-structures, are correspondingly scarce. It is this characteristic, no doubt, which led Richard Katz to speak of '. . . the lapidary style . . . Each sentence expresses shortly and clearly *one* idea.'

On the vocabulary side, Remarque, we have seen, grounds his language on the precisely factual word. Yet he also has a command of overtones: As [critic] O.M. Fontana observed when the novel appeared, 'Erich Maria Remarque has what [the German novelist] Ludwig Renn lacks: words——words that give more than a photograph—words with all the fine resonances and movements of the soul, of atmosphere, of the inexpressible, imperceptible as these are to the factual sense—in short, poetic words. Some of these effects, we have noted, spring from juxtaposition, of war and nature, or of the physical and the spiritual; others from metaphor, which is kept simple and sensuous. Liedloff comments on the colloquialisms and 'soldier-language expressions'. Remarque also has a line in brash similes:

> He [Tjaden] is thin when he sits down to eat, and when he gets up again, he's as fat as a pregnant bug . . .
>
> Even his [dying Kemmerich's] voice sounds like ashes.
>
> When Kat stands back at the hut and says: 'We're for it—', well, that's his opinion; but when he says it up here, the phrase has the sharpness of a bayonet in the moonlight, it cuts through our thoughts . . .

Liedloff comments on such features: 'Such expressions are proper in the actual conversation but bothersome in the narrative because they disrupt its unity.' A few lines later he speaks of 'Remarque's opinion'. But he misdirects himself here. What he sees as a weakness is in fact a strength, as Klein has already argued. The style of the book is not Remarque's style, and the opinions are not Remarque's opinions; at least, not in the first instance. From the beginning of Chapter I until two paragraphs from the end of Chapter XII, the novel is narrated by the central figure, Paul Bäumer. This narrative stance provides Remarque with a realistic context for a naive and simple style, which is part of the novel's popular appeal; but also for a fragmented, uncoordinated syntax, and for the use of the present tense with its immediacy; these features thus become part of the famous 'frog's eye view' of the war. He is able to give the short-sighted comments on events of Paul Bäumer himself, and through him of the other characters, without the need to ' provide an omniscient narrative perspective—indeed, with a requirement *not* to do so. In short, style and point of view are matched, and both reflect the incomprehensibility of war.

REMARQUE'S EFFECTIVE CHOICE OF NARRATOR

The choice of a first-person narrator does however create one possible problem. The two concluding paragraphs have to stem from a new, apparently omniscient third-person narrator, whose intervention is needed after the first-person narrator's death. Strangely, however, the novel does not suffer from this change of viewpoint; nor from the absence of any explanation of the mechanics by which it came to be set down—an absence which distinguishes *All Quiet* from Goethe's *Werther*, with which in narrative standpoint as in other ways it has close affinities. The introductory paragraph preceding Chapter I may, perhaps, best be considered as a kind of epigraph, or even foreword, rather than as part of the novel proper; which may be another way of expressing Klein's parallel with the short captions at the beginning and end of films.

Narrative viewpoint leads us on to consider characters. *All Quiet* focuses on Paul Bäumer, his former classmates, and—to secure some age-variation—a few fellow-soldiers of different background, notably Stanislaus Katczinsky. Klein's argument that the central figure is closely connected with only *two* others (Katczinsky and Kropp), however, seems to have been influenced by a desire for symmetry with *Her Privates We*; at least as strong a case could be made out for Tjaden as for Kropp, and the model in *All Quiet* is not so much a triangle as a series of concentric circles around Bäumer, with Katczinsky on the innermost of them. But Klein rightly points out that Remarque's choice of characters successfully solves the problem of identity which faces the authors of war novels, whilst at the same time creating a curiously unrealistic cross-section of the fighting troops, with no senior officers and hardly any junior ones or N.C.O.s. This again is a powerful determinant of the sense of alienation which pervades the novel.

Paul Bäumer, sensitive, an intellectual and an artist by inclination, trying without complete success to grow a thicker skin, may be seen as a distant descendant of Werther, with whose semi-anagrammatic name his own name may have affinities.

THE NOVEL'S STRUCTURE

Narrative viewpoint and the focus on the central character are also closely linked with structure. At one level, the work is divided into many small sections, separated by asterisks: 92 of them, which gives an average length, in the original edition, of about three sides. This again is a feature that makes for easy reading; but, combined with the predominance of the present tense, it also makes for a realistic effect—that of a journal entry or a brief conversation. A journalistic approach has been adopted for aesthetic effect.

Yet the fact that the novel has twelve chapters suggests that its underlying structure is not that of a string of casual jottings. Liedloff's analysis starts from the observation that Chapters VI (38 pages) and VII (48 pages) are much longer than the other chapters (average 19.6 pages); and he argues that these chapters are the centre of the book: VI, because it is the fullest depiction of battle in the novel, and VII because it shows the characters relaxing after their period in the line. Liedloff's suggestion that the novel is built around these two chapters is resisted by Klein, who argues that the structure is cyclical: Chapters VII to XII repeat the sequence of I to VI, with one important difference—there is no escape at the end of the second series. Another, small-scale, example of the cyclical principle at work would be Chapters IV and V, the wire-carrying followed by the goose-roasting. The novel operates structurally, in fact, on an alternation between the cruelty and despair of the battle-scenes, and a gradual return to life during periods in reserve. Chapters VI and VII are the major instance of this alternation; but, ironically, the fact that Paul and his friends escape from this battle is not a guarantee that they will escape from the war; the second half of the novel moves inexorably to their destruction. This process, which is intensified by the changeover from single events to iterative formulae, to which Klein has drawn attention, is also accompanied by seasonal changes. Like *Werther*, *All Quiet* occupies two summers and two autumns, handled in such a way that Chapters I to VI seem to be all in summer, and Chapters VII to XII all in autumn: like *Werther*, if less formally, this novel too is in two contrasting books.

INCREASING ALIENATION

The progression of the novel is thus one of increasing alienation from any world but that of war. This alienation is implicit, and indeed explicit, at the beginning, but the characters still behave as if they can escape, whatever they may say. Paul himself hopes for a miracle in the love-scene in Chapter VII, but it is hard to believe that he finds one, except for the existential moment. And the sterility of his leave: coming, as it does, after the big battle, it should celebrate his safety, but instead it confirms his despair. So the structure of the novel articulates its themes.

The most basic of these is the monstrous unacceptability of modern trench warfare—manifest especially in Chapter VI. A second theme is the moral bankruptcy of leaders who have encouraged young men to volunteer for this holocaust—expressed already in the discussion of their form-master Kantorek in Chapter I. Yet a third theme is the suggestion that, when the war is over, something must be done to change the world we live in—intimated, for example, in the Duval scene in Chapter IX. More important is the 'lost generation' theme, already sounded in the book's epigraph:

> This book is meant neither as an indictment nor as a confession. It is meant only to try to report on a generation that was destroyed by the War—even when it escaped the shells.

The sense of comradeship which awareness of belonging to a 'lost generation' engenders is yet another theme. And finally, there is the existential theme of the assertion of self, in the face of the nothingness of war, through sensual experience and through contact with nature—a theme which gradually fades from the novel as alienation becomes more pervasive.

TRUE TO LIFE

The narrative standpoint of *All Quiet* does not allow these themes to be fully reconciled with one another, or even to be fully articulated. It is also true, as many critics have observed, that Paul Bäumer and his friends are not, as he claims and the novel implies, representative of the effect on all soldiers of trench warfare and its horrors. And yet, it is wrong to demand, either, as Remarque's Nationalist critics did, that these victims should have been more heroic, or, as Marxist critics do, that they should have been more consciously revolutionary. What Remarque achieves is more true to life than either of these: a depiction of mean sensual man, crushed by circumstances and yet preserving his humanity in unexpected ways. It is this that, ultimately, captured his readers; and it is this, and the unobtrusive formal mastery with which he achieves it, that is at the heart of his literary value. Like all major writers, he shows us what is wrong with our world, not how to put it right.

Paul Bäumer Is a Christ Figure

Edwin M. Moseley

At the time he wrote *Pseudonyms of Christ*, from which this selection is excerpted, Edwin M. Moseley was a long-time English professor at Skidmore College in Saratoga Springs, New York. In this book, he analyzes a number of novels which have protagonists who remind him in some way of Christ, either because they are saviors or martyrs. Moseley views Paul Bäumer, the narrator of *All Quiet*, as the latter. Like Christ, and like many young men of the World War I generation, he is sacrificed for the political "sins" of others. Moseley sees other parallels with Christ as well.

Remarque's *All Quiet on the Western Front* . . . achieves a . . . paradox of softness in the midst of harshness. In this sense it is strikingly different from the number of war novels that are basically stories of the development of youth from naïve commitment to experienced detachment. Hemingway's *A Farewell to Arms*, a great novel on many levels, is an example of the initiation story in which the innocent in the modern world learns that he is vulnerable to hurt by an indifferent universe and that the length of his survival depends on deliberate protection against vulnerability. To be sure, Hemingway's characters are always questing love, a home, religion, order, but they do not find them because they are unwilling to admit that suffering and sacrifice are essential to achieved commitment. The structure of the book is tight: a step by step journey from innocence to experience. And the style is economic in keeping with the theme of the advisability of hiding the emotions from a world which will torture them.

All Quiet makes basically the same points as *A Farewell to Arms*, but its methods are totally unlike Hemingway's and its

From *Pseudonyms of Christ in the Modern Novel: Motifs and Methods*, by Edwin M. Moseley; © 1962 by University of Pittsburgh. Reprinted by permission of the University of Pittsburgh Press.

mood is different. Remarque's constant refrain is literally: "We are a lost generation," we who were too young to have roots in experience and who have discovered that the words intended as roots by parents, teachers, preachers, politicians have no relationship to experience. Remarque's hero is nineteen when the book begins and twenty when he dies, and he has a strong feeling that even the men of twenty-five who have wives and children of their own have a sense of something to return to. In one scene the soldiers typically discuss what they will do when the peace comes, but with a sense that the young men dragged out of school into war have had no chance even to create the lies by which men live in peacetime. Now, facing the truth of death so soon, they are denied the years of illusion which are the luxury of living before every man faces the heart of darkness and makes his individual adjustment to it.

Remarque's protagonist Paul, who tells his own story, is constantly surprised that at the age of nineteen he has, as Hemingway might put it, "lived with death a long time." According to Paul, his journey of learning was practically completed in his "first bombardment." In that moment, "the world as they [the older generation] taught it to us broke in pieces . . . we saw that there was nothing of their world left. We were all at once terribly alone; and alone we must see it through." For the archetypal sacrificial heroes, death and the aloneness with which one faces it come at the end of the epic drama, but Paul in effect begins with them. This consciousness of the shocking shortening of the journey of learning is forever with us in the novel. It is in every episode, and it is in image after image. In a day a child moves from innocence to experience. In a year a young man moves from maturity to death. At the climax of the novel Paul moves across a foxhole to a French soldier whom he has killed because he had to:

> I drag myself toward him, hesitate, support myself on my hands, creep a bit farther, wait, again a terrible journey of three yards, a long, a terrible journey.

This is the most telling image of the book, "a terrible journey of three yards," a life shortened in space as throughout the novel it is shortened in time.

A LIFETIME IN 300 PAGES

Here is indeed the essence of art. Selection, the symbolic short cut, careful manipulation of structure allow us to live a lifetime in two hours in the theater or through thirty pages or a thousand in fiction. It is literally time and space that are shortened for us so that we suspend our disbelief and accept the eternal and the universal which endure beyond all time and space. . . .

All Quiet achieves its disregard of time through a kind of lyric method. Paul, the protagonist, tells his story in an almost impressionistic manner. He moves back and forth in time from the present moment to past moments as details of the present suggest episodes of the past to him. He moves between the description of action and the lyrical expression of feelings and evaluations. The events that evolve *can* be placed in time and space, but this is not important: the effect is lyrical and tender, not epic and grand, the emotional expression of a moment to which a lifetime has been reduced. In structure, as in that of so many first novels, *All Quiet* seems loose, unpolished, youthful, but it *is* youthful and therein is both its failure and its success as art.

In one passage of the kind of lyricism to which I refer, Paul is speaking:

> It is chilly. I am on sentry and stare into the darkness. My strength is exhausted as always after an attack, and so it is hard for me to be alone with my thoughts. They are not properly thoughts; they are memories which in my weakness turn homeward and strangely move me.

> The parachute-lights shoot upwards—and I see a picture, a summer evening. I am in a cathedral cloister and look at the tall rose trees that bloom in the middle of the little cloister garden where the monks lie buried. Around the walls are the stone carvings of the Stations of the Cross. No one is there. A great quietness rules in this blossoming quadrangle, the sun lies warm on the heavy grey stones. I place my hand upon them and feel the warmth. At the right-hand corner the green cathedral spire ascends into the pale blue sky of the evening. Between the glowing columns of the cloister is the cool darkness that only churches have, and I stand there and wonder whether, when I am twenty, I shall have experienced the bewildering emotions of love.

> The image is alarmingly near; it touches me before it dissolves in the light of the next star-shell.

DEATH AS A WAY TO LIFE

The Stations of the Cross is a correlative to which the reader responds intuitively, and I respond to it deliberately as well in terms of the Christ-motif in which I have been interested. For the moment, follow these responses, the intuitive and the deliberate one, and see where they lead us. When we come across the direct reference to Christ, we think with a feeling akin to *pieta* of the plight of Paul and the other young men being sacrificed in the war. We may think too of the young men bearing the cross for an entire society which with good or bad intentions has condemned them to die. We think, in this passage at least, of death as a way to life, for the imagery of the passage is that of growth and regeneration: rose trees blooming in the night, a "blossoming quadrangle" of stone still warm with the day's sun, a green spire reaching upward into a blue sky. Or we may think on the other hand of a kind of lost Eden for which Paul longs in a world of death. In the paragraph which follows, Paul himself describes the memory as a "calm" one, but a calmness against which he must protect himself lest he drop his defenses against the everlasting "unquietness" of the front.

Or more deliberately: The Stations of the Cross which Paul recalls having seen in a cathedral garden were the pictorial representations, sometimes in painting, sometimes as here in bas-relief, of Christ's "journey" from his condemnation to death up to the point at which his body was laid in the tomb. Church lore differs as to how many "stations" there actually were, but most representations suggest the following fourteen: (1) Christ is condemned to death; (2) the cross is laid upon him; (3) he falls for the first time; (4) he meets his Blessed Mother; (5) Simon of Cyrene is made to bear the cross; (6) Christ's face is wiped by Veronica; (7) he falls for the second time; (8) he meets the women of Jerusalem; (9) he falls for the third time; (10) he is stripped of his garments; (11) he is crucified; (12) he dies on the cross; (13) his body is taken down from the cross; (14) his body is laid in the tomb. In the Middle Ages a definite ritual developed around these picturizations whereby the devotee went in effect on a miniature vicarious pilgrimage along the way Christ traversed in Jerusalem from Pilate's house to Mount Calvary. The more fortunate devout of course actually made the trip to Jerusalem and traversed in person the "Via Dolorosa," as the way of the cross became known.

Sorrow Is the Way

Remarque's reader soon thinks of the way of the cross again, for on the very next page Paul says that the way of those who have roots is the way of nostalgia, but for himself and the

A TRIBUTE TO YOUTH

A review of All Quiet on the Western Front *published in the* American Mercury *(August 1929) asserted that the novel depicts "the indomitable spirit of youth."*

"All Quiet on the Western Front" ... is by no means a mere tract against war: it is rather a gorgeous and epical paean to the indomitable spirit of youth—an overwhelmingly eloquent celebration of the high courage and resolution that make war possible, and are evoked to the same extent by no other demand upon *Homo sapiens.* The German boy of this story wonders what it is all about, but he is no less heroic for wondering. There is in him and his comrades a fortitude that shows in the end an almost majestic character; they cease to be youngsters wallowing in the mud and become personages out of a tragedy in the grand manner. It is surely no discredit to the human race that it can produce such men, and it is surely no argument against war that they die in vain. All heroes, at bottom, die in vain, whether in war or in peace. The rewards of life go to those prudent enough to live on.

other lost ones, "these memories of former times do not awaken desire so much as sorrow—a strange, apprehensible melancholy." The way of his generation, like the way of Christ bearing the cross, *is* the way of sorrow. The very imagery of the journey is with us once more:

Today we could pass through the scenes of our youth like travellers. ... We long to be there; but could we live there?

We are forlorn like children, and experienced like old men, we are crude and sorrowful and superficial—I believe we are lost.

Paul's journey, then, like Christ's, is the "via dolorosa," the way from the condemnation to death, to the actual death on the last page of the novel. This is not as far as we can deliberately go with the image, the Stations of the Cross. It would be an interesting piece of craftsmanship if, say, the steps of Paul's journey to his death were symbolically those of Christ, ... but in this book Remarque is not that kind of a writer. Having taken the Stations of the Cross as a correlative, one might relate the gambling for Christ's garments to Remarque's motif of: Who will get the dead man's shoes? The removing of the shoes from the dying is an age-old folk motif that can be read on as many levels as, say, Oedipus, and in some versions its implications are not unlike those of the

soldiers' desiring Christ's robe without respect for his death.
But in *All Quiet* the claiming of the clothes of the dead men is
not part of any structure analogous to the traditional structure
of Christ's Stations. Remarque's structure, as we have said, is
more lyrical and associative than narrative and logical.

The Stations of the Cross, then, is a dominant image at a piv-
otal point, but neither a key to overall structure nor a part of
any cluster of images more specific than the broad sacrificial-
hero ones. We have mentioned before a possible difference
between integrated meanings and parallel ones. The difference is not always valid, but pursuit of the parallel as if it
were an integral part of the whole quickly points up the pre-
cariously parasitic and absurd nature of literary criticism. I
admit my own tendency toward critical venturing. In the
light of my own interest in the Christ patterns of the novels
in which I had at first *intuitively* discovered them, I *did* look
up Stations of the Cross. The sources which I read with interest listed the "stations" or steps in Christ's final journey to
death in much the same way as I have above and besides discussed the derivation of the word *station.* A *station,* according to one source, is a fast of bread and water, whereby as
pilgrims we simulate the suffering of Christ. Even in this
sense, it may come from a military metaphor that occurs
several times in the Bible as, for example, in ". . . we are also
God's soldiers," the Latin word for soldier or military guard
having been *statio.* Ah, I said, *station . . . soldier . . . also
God's soldiers . . .* Remarque's soldier Paul. Another source
referred station more directly to *stationarius,* "a military encampment," and then figuratively, "an encampment protect-
ing one from the assaults of the devil." Again, *station . . .* the
place in which we *stand* to repel the enemy . . . the manifold
irony that the word *enemy* has taken on by Remarque's last
page. True, creative writing demands creative reading, but
the obligation of the reader is to be imaginative *within* the
limits of the book. Parallels are interesting and enlightening,
but pursuing them is like playing a game for which there are
no rules: it's both too easy and too hard.

One is tempted to play a similar game with the name
Paul. . . . Does an awareness of the Biblical Paul's preaching
of fellowship enrich young Paul's refrain that the "finest
thing that arose out of the war" was "comradeship"? Coinci-
dentally and significantly, yes, but hardly because Remarque was using the name Paul as a guide to meaning.

DEATH AND COMMUNION

Comradeship in the face of death is essentially a religious idea, and Remarque handles it as such throughout his novel. Communion as a kind of holy eating together by way of transcending the death to which men are damned is a dominant image of the book. There is a wonderful scene in which Paul and Kat, the older man who serves as a kind of natural mentor to Paul and his group, eat a goose they have stolen in a previous comic episode. They eat, and two men who "formerly . . . should not have had a single thought in common . . . sit with a goose between us and feel in unison, and are so intimate that we do not even speak. . . . I love him. . . . We are brothers and press on one another the choicest pieces." Later, in a deserted village to which Paul, Kat, and others are assigned, there is a long, happy last eating scene before Paul is wounded. In the last narrative action of the book Paul carries the wounded Kat back to the post. On the way Paul thinks that Kat has fainted, but when he arrives, he discovers that his burden has been hit in the head with a splinter. Paul has saved Kat only to have him die. An orderly, noticing Paul's stunned response, asks: "You are not related, are you?" "No, we are not related. No, we are not related," Paul thinks with all of the ironic awareness that every man is related to every other man. This Paul like the other one preached fellowship with those in the same plight with himself.

If all men are brothers, who then is the enemy? Paul looks at Russian prisoners through a barbed wire fence. He knows that the very "word of command" which has made them enemies can transform them into friends. He is frightened, for to think in that way lies "the abyss." If he is to survive, he must repress these thoughts until after the war has ended. Then, perhaps, pursuing them, he might give purpose to his questless life. Paul breaks his cigarettes in half and shares them with the Russians; he gives them part of the cakes his mother has made for him.

The scene with the Russians is preparation for the climax of the book which we have already mentioned in another connection. Paul, lost from his patrol, is hiding in a foxhole. He stabs a retreating Frenchman who falls into the hole beside him. Watching him die, Paul at last makes the "terrible journey" of three yards across the bottom of the hole till he is beside his victim. By three o'clock the man is dead. After all, Paul's maturation turns out not to have been completed in that first bombardment. Never before has he seen a man die whom he, Paul, has killed with his own hands. Throughout the book Paul and his friends have blamed worldwide diplomats, the Kaiser, the generals, the manufacturers, the parents, the preachers, the teachers for their plight in the war, but now Paul takes responsibility for the sins of man in which he has participated. "Forgive me, comrade; how could you be my enemy? If we threw away these rifles and this uniform you could be my brother just like Kat." Paul swears a life of penance and sacrifice for the death of the man whose life has been bound up in some mysterious way with his own life. He promises to devote himself after the war to helping his "enemy's" family. He has crucified a stranger, and he *will* suffer for this greatest of all sins.

TRUTH, DEATH, AND LIFE

But back in the trenches with his own men, he is reassured and comforted. "After all, war is war." Business is business, and life is life. This is the conscious world where the devil rules. To deny it, that is, to pursue the godhead, is martyrdom on behalf of one's brothers. That way lies "the abyss," according to convention and the devil. But according to the godhead which Paul would imitate if he could, that way is salvation. What Paul learns in his journey for a moment and for all time is that man cannot pursue the truth and live. Of course, as Hemingway says, if he does not pursue it, he dies too, but only a little later. The joker is that the early death in the cause of truth may be the one way to the everlasting life.

The Structure of *All Quiet* Helps Carry Out the Theme of Alienation

Christine R. Barker and R.W. Last

All Quiet is written to resemble the diary of Paul
Bäumer, depicting the day-to-day lives of himself
and his comrades. Yet it is not merely a series of
events, say Christine R. Barker and R.W. Last.
Remarque has very carefully crafted the novel as a
series of juxtapositions—light and dark, somber and
humorous. These antitheses help carry out the
theme of alienation. For example, as he contrasts the
young men's pasts as students and sons with their
present as soldiers subject to the whims of officers
and the war's events, it becomes clear that his characters are alienated from their past—and from their
future. They live only in the present.

Barker and Last's book, from which this viewpoint
is taken, is one of the few that analyze *All Quiet* in
detail.

Although the novel is divided into twelve chapters of varying
length, they do not necessarily point to more than one facet of
the basic structure of *Im Westen nichts Neues*. In this novel he
is introducing a structural technique—which he was to refine
in his subsequent works—which involves a series of small
episodes as building bricks, not necessarily related to one another causally (that is to say, the "plot" is not particularly important), but cumulative in effect. Bäumer's account is very
much like a diary, consisting in the main of either description
of a sequence of events or internal monologue, without link-
ing passages of any kind. It is, one might say, without seeking
to over-stretch the comparison, a kind of "Stationenroman"
on the lines of the Brechtian epic theatre with its "Stationen-
dramen", that is, a novel held together, not by the traditional

From *Erich Maria Remarque*, by Christine R. Barker and R.W. Last. Copyright © 1979
Oswald Wolff. Reprinted with permission of Barnes & Noble.

glue of a developing action culminating in a climax and de-
nouement, but rather by broader thematic links, such as character or ideas. And, as far as Remarque's novels in general are
concerned, there is a strange inverse relationship between
their literary quality and the tightness of their plot.

Im Westen nichts Neues falls into three parts plus a contemplative interlude. The first part (Chapters I–VI) explores
the experiences of the private soldier at the front and behind
the lines, together with reflections back on home, the last
days in school and life in the training barracks. It opens with
a depleted company newly returned from the front, only
eighty men out of a hundred and fifty, and concludes in similar vein with the return of another company, this time reduced to a mere thirty-two men. The central section (Chapter VII, the longest in the book) deals partly with women,
aspirations towards a world of love beyond the war, and
partly with Bäumer's disastrous experience of leave, when
he fails to regain contact with his past. There then follows a
contemplative interlude (Chapter VIII), principally devoted
to Bäumer's thoughts as he stands guard over a group of
Russian prisoners of war; in this section, he actually pon-
ders on the wider political and moral issues raised by the
armed conflict (not a few critics must have had faulty copies
of *Im Westen nichts Neues* with these particular pages ex-
punged!). In the final section (Chapters IX–XII), the action
becomes more concentrated: vignettes of fellow soldiers,
each ending in their death, are sandwiched between periods
of reflection and contemplation, and the narrative technique—unusually for Remarque—switches over from
blocks of description and action with a high content of dialogue to a summarized, compressed account of the concluding phase of the war, as time seems to become suspended
and the comrades' emotions utterly numbed. And, at the
end, Bäumer dies, just as peace is approaching.

THE NOVEL IS SKILLFULLY PACED

Reading critics of *Im Westen nichts Neues*, one might all too
readily gain the impression that the novel is a succession of
nightmarish situations and unrelieved gloom, but this is far
from being the case. Remarque skillfully paces the development of the action, interposing scenes of real happiness and
contentment, some of which contain episodes that are extremely funny. On one such occasion, Bäumer clumsily

attempts to "liberate" a brace of geese from a farmyard; he is cornered by the farm bulldog and pinned to the ground by that animal; and, finally, he manages to extricate his revolver:

> When I get my revolver in my hand, it starts to shake. I press my hand on to the ground and tell myself: raise the revolver, fire before the dog can get at me and make myself scarce. Slowly I take my breath and calm down. Then, holding my breath, I jerk the revolver into the air, it goes off, the dog leaps yowling to one side, I reach the stable door and go head over heels over one of the geese which had fled from me.

So he makes a grab for it, hurls it over the wall to Kat, who puts the bird out of its misery; and Bäumer joins them, having just escaped the fangs of the frustrated bulldog. . . .

Another amusing episode which is equally concerned with food, but this time, so to speak, from a different point of view, relates to the inevitable outcome of gastronomic excess. Kat manages to acquire two sucking pigs, and these are roasted with all the trimmings:

> We fall asleep chewing. But things get bad in the night. We have eaten too much fat. Fresh roast sucking pig has a devastating effect on the bowels. There is an incessant to-ing and fro-ing in the dugout. Men are squatting about outside in twos and threes with their trousers down, cursing. Getting on for four in the morning we achieve a record: all eleven men . . . on their haunches outside together.

Even the tyrannical corporal Himmelstoss gives occasion for some amusement, as when the soldiers obey his orders with excessive slowness, thus whipping him into a hoarse frenzy; but there is a grimmer side to the humour, too, both in the scene where Himmelstoss is swathed in a sheet and beaten by the vengeful group of comrades, and when their ex-teacher Kantorek is also humiliated by a former pupil of his in the barracks when the rôles are reversed and Kantorek is actually a subordinate to his erstwhile student.

ALTERNATING LIGHT AND DARKNESS

Such episodes, however, are not scattered randomly about the novel; in this, as in all else, Remarque pays considerable attention to the detailed organization of his material. Opening on a positive note, the novel alternates light and dark episodes, the intensity of both increasing as the narrative progresses. In Chapter I, the comrades sit *al fresco* on latrine buckets in a circle playing cards in a scene of tranquil contentment; and this sequence is closely followed by a visit to the dying Kemmerich. Chapter V brings the *contretemps* with the goose, which is then consumed with considerable relish in an atmosphere of peace and fulfilment; and this comes just before the comrades move up to the front line past coffins piled high in readiness for the victims of the coming offensive. And, finally, in Chapter X there is a sequence in an evacuated village—"an idyll of guzzling and sleeping"—which they are supposed to be guarding, and where they have been left more or less to their own devices; and this is immediately followed by Bäumer and Kropp sustaining wounds in action. Each of the positive scenes, it will have been noted, is concerned with basic functions of the human body. . . .

Similarly, Remarque establishes a series of contrasts between scenes at the front and behind the lines, in an alternating sequence in which more and more stress comes to be placed on the front as the struggle becomes grimmer and the small group of comrades finds its numbers gradually whittled down. This aspect of the novel's structure is reflected in the chapter endings, each of which—with the exception of the Russian prisoners interlude in Chapter VIII—is concerned with a departure or a return of some kind, and the novel ends with the final departure from this life by Bäumer.

The process being depicted is one of a decreasing freedom of action and a growing sense of claustrophobia; there is, it becomes increasingly evident, no way out save through death. This relentless crushing of life and the closing in of death is underlined by the motif of Kemmerich's English flying boots. At the beginning of the novel, he lies dying, one leg amputated, and Müller is obsessed with the desire to inherit them. When Kemmerich realizes that he is close to death, he hands them over to Müller. When the latter dies in Chapter XI and Bäumer comes into their possession, we know that he too is marked for death. Of the original group of eight comrades, only one remains, Tjaden, and he in turn inherits the boots; but "Tjaden has luck as always" and he alone also will survive, despite the ill-fated boots, and indeed he reappears in the sequel *Der Weg zurück*.

SERIES OF ANTITHESES

The whole of *Im Westen nichts Neues* is in fact based on a series of antitheses which reflect various levels of alienation in the minds of the small and dwindling band of comrades. The first of these to come to light is that between "them" and "us":

Whilst they were still writing and speechifying, we saw field hospitals and dying men;—whilst they were proclaiming service of the state as the highest good, we knew already that fear of death is the stronger. This did not turn us into rebels, deserters, or cowards—all these words came so readily to their lips—we loved our homeland just as much as they did, and we advanced bravely with every attack;—but . . . we had suddenly had our eyes opened. And we saw that of their world nothing remained.

There are two immediate consequences that flow from this gulf: the first is that the private soldiers form a closed and self-contained group, that is, they acquire and foster a sense of "comradeship" which dominates every aspect of their existence, but not in the meaning of the word coined by the National Socialists: this is not a case of the "Frontgemeinschaft" (brotherhood of the front) which is such a key concept in their interpretation of the rôle of the First World War, far from it. It is, rather, a negative state, a protective shrinking within a cocoon of intense intimacy with fellow soldiers as an essential means towards self-preservation and the maintenance of sanity in a world gone mad. After being lost for endless hours in No Man's Land, Bäumer hears the voices of his comrades who are out searching for him:

An uncommon warmth flows through me all of a sudden. Those voices, those few, softly-spoken words, those footsteps in the trench to my rear suddenly wrench me out of the terrible isolation of the mortal fear to which I had all but succumbed. Those voices mean more to me than my life . . . they are the most powerful and protective thing that there can ever be: they are the voices of my comrades.

SENSE OF BELONGING IS LOST

The second consequence of the gulf between "them" and "us" is that the comrades have lost all sense of belonging to that hierarchy of rôles that sustained them as they grew up: father, mother, schoolmaster and the rest have forfeited their validity; and a new hierarchy has come to be established within the confines of the closed group of comrades. In *Im Westen nichts Neues*, it is Kat, twice the age of the others, who acts out the rôle of the father: he is the source of authority, the leader, the indestructible one, whose death by a stray piece of shrapnel as Bäumer is carrying him to a field station to have his wounds dressed so poignantly parallels the wasting away of Bäumer's disease-stricken mother at home. Parent substitute and "real" parent are now both irretrievably lost. (Of Bäumer's father we hear virtually nothing, save that he is a bookbinder; and the French soldier Gérard Duval, whom Bäumer stabs in a crater in No Man's Land, and who dies slowly and in great pain before his eyes, also followed that trade.)

Significantly, Kat's qualities are vastly different from those of the group's parents and other figures of authority: he is admired for his ability both to survive in a cruel environment and to care for the needs of his comrades. This finds its sharpest expression in relation to his skill at conjuring food and other necessities of life apparently out of empty air. And so it is hardly surprising to find Bäumer writing about Kat in these terms when he wakens in the night during a rest-break after a wire-laying party, frightened by a sudden sound:

> It is so strange, am I a child? . . . and then I recognize Katczinsky's silhouette. He is sitting there quietly, the old soldier . . . I sit upright: I feel strangely alone. It is good that Kat is there.

And again, as the captured goose is being roasted in the gathering gloom, Bäumer falls into a reverie and is roused by Kat:

> Is my face wet, and where am I? Kat stands before me, his giant shadow bent over me like home.

But, for Kat, as for the rest of them, "home" is the barracks; and the nostalgic reminiscences of the group are directed, not back at their schooldays and childhood, but towards their experiences in the training barracks, when, for example, the order was given for piano-players to take two paces forward, and the unfortunates who did so were briskly marched off to the cookhouse for spud-bashing; or when Himmelstoss made them practise time and again what he evidently regarded as the difficult art of "changing trains in Löhne", which meant that they were obliged to crawl beneath their beds—which served to simulate the underpass at the station—and emerge smartly on the other side.

CUT OFF FROM PAST

Thus a second area of alienation is on the temporal plane. The little group of comrades is effectively cut off from the past: "Since we have been here, our earlier life has been excluded from us, without our having done anything to bring that about". The years prior to the outbreak of war, and the values and knowledge which the comrades had acquired then have no meaning for them now. "Between today and the past there is a gulf . . . it is a different world." The past is an alien realm to which they could return only as strangers. It

FROM SCHOOL TO THE TRENCHES

A.F. Bance points out in a 1977 essay written for the Modern Language Review *that the soldiers of* All Quiet on the Western Front *lost all touch with the larger world and lived only in the present of the war.*

Remarque's generation is the one that was just old enough at the beginning of the war to go straight from school into the trenches. Its experience, Remarque claims, is more shattering, its fate more pathetic than that of others slightly older or slightly younger (the former had already established the basis of an existence before the war, the latter escaped the same total exposure to it). In other war novels, characters are revealed, and perhaps warped, but not, as in *Im Westen*, entirely formed by the war situation. For Remarque's youngsters the war is a total experience, it is *the* experience (again we are reminded of Hitler's speeches) which imprints itself on a *tabula rasa*. War becomes the only point of reference in a world that is otherwise totally incomprehensible.

is as if the past has died; and, in order to underline this, Remarque twice employs the image of the photograph: when Kemmerich is expiring of his wounds in the hospital bed, he is described as looking blurred and indeterminate in outline, "like a photographic plate which has been double exposed", just a hazy shadow of the man he once was. And this image recurs when Bäumer is on guard duty in the darkness reflecting back on the scenes and experiences of his younger days and recognizes that, for him, they are irretrievably lost:

> It would be just like pondering over a photograph of a dead comrade; it is his features, it is his face, and the days we spent together would acquire a deceptive life in our memory, but it is not the thing itself.

In the front line, what they learned in school is utterly useless to them. At one point, the comrades joke about the knowledge they acquired in school, throwing the old questions at one another: "How many inhabitants has Melbourne?" "What were the goals of the Göttinger Hain?" (A circle of sentimental eighteenth-century poets.) "How many children has Charles the Bold?"

> We can't remember very much about all that rubbish. Nor has it been of any use to us. No one taught us in school how to light a cigarette under attack in the rain, how to make a fire with wet wood—or that the best place to thrust a bayonette is

in the stomach, because it doesn't get stuck fast there like it does in the ribs.

On entering the army, they were thoroughly brainwashed into forgetting their previous scale of values, although these simply lay dormant at first; it was not until their exposure to front-line fighting over an extended period of time that they became obliterated altogether. In another example of Remarque's skilful use of theme and variation, the recruits were taught "that a polished button is more important than four volumes of Schopenhauer". This is then neatly stood on its head in the sequence where Bäumer is observing to his amusement his former schoolmaster Kantorek being drilled in the barracks square by his former pupil, Mittelstaedt, who cries out: "Landsturmmann Kantorek, is that what you call cleaning buttons? You never seem to learn. Unsatisfactory, Kantorek, unsatisfactory". He turns the schoolmaster's words against him, destroying all the man's values in a sour act of revenge for the fact that Kantorek, in encouraging his pupils to enlist, had caused precisely the same fate to befall them. This rupture with the past is one of the dominant themes of Remarque's work, the discontinuity of life, this jolting from one plane of existence to another for which man is completely unprepared.

CUT OFF FROM FUTURE

Not only are they cut off from the past; a gulf also extends between them and the future. The inability of those who survive the war to readjust to peacetime conditions is suggested by the way in which Bäumer, walking along the streets of his home town while on leave, starts with fright at the screeching sound of the tramcars, mistaking the noise for that of a grenade whistling through the air. The knowledge they have acquired in the trenches is as useless to them in time of peace as their school lessons in time of war.

Only those of the older generation, like Kat, will be able to slip back more or less unscarred into civilian life, since they came to war as mature adults, with a firm foundation in life, and they have something to build on when they return; Kat, for example, has his wife and, significantly, a young son to provide hope for the future. But, as Bäumer writes of his own generation: "The war has ruined us for everything". They have been caught up in the war when the hold of school and parents was slackening, but before they had had the opportunity to enter upon adult life: none are married, none have a job, none know which direction they want their future to take.

The young comrades feel equally alienated from the political and social issues of the day; it is not "their" war, and they can see no sense in the notion, say, of a nation actually wanting to attack another nation, a personification of abstractions which, to them, is nonsensical. And when the Kaiser himself appears to review the troops, their reaction is one of bemused disappointment; surely he cannot be the much-vaunted embodiment of the highest ideals of the German nation, they ask themselves; and this leads them on to challenge the whole question of the war, its origins and objectives. In the end, Albert Kropp speaks for them all when he bursts out: "It's better not to talk about all this nonsense at all".

CUT OFF FROM REALITY

Worse still, they feel cut off from reality itself and from their own humanity by the horrific routine of death and suffering in the trenches. They come to lose all sense of time,

> and all that keeps us going is the fact that there are even weaker . . . yet more helpless men who look up at us with wide-open eyes as gods who are able for a while to evade death.

All they possess is life and freedom from injury. They have even lost all sense of their youthful vitality:

> Iron youth. Youth! None of us is more than twenty years old. But young? Youth? That's way back in the past. We are old men.

And in the trenches they are coming to discover that even life itself does not belong to them. At the very beginning of the novel, when Kemmerich is dying, it is stressed that the life has already drained out of him, that "the face already bears the alien lines" of death, that "there is no life pulsing under the skin any more", that he has the mark of death upon him. When Kemmerich has expired, Bäumer's reaction is one of terrible exultation, for he is alive, he has life within him, and he is filled with the most powerful desire to cling on to that elusive force whatever the cost:

> Streams of energy flow through the earth, surging up into me through the soles of my feet . . . My limbs move freely, I feel my joints strong . . . The night lives, I live. I feel a hunger, more powerful than for mere food.

The ground is frequently referred to in *Im Westen nichts Neues* as the source of a life-giving power, and the strength and significance of the "life force"—which has been conveniently overlooked by the critics—lies at the heart of all Remarque's mature work, and, as we shall see, it is a concept which he develops in the novels which follow upon *Im Westen nichts Neues.* One of them, *Der Funke Leben* (meaning: the spark of life) has the life force as its central theme, and the title of this novel, which explores the power of life in the midst of death and torture in the concentration camps, is prefigured in the scene where the goose is being roasted, and Bäumer describes Kat and himself as "two tiny sparks of life" in the darkness.

So when Bäumer and his comrades state that "we want to live at any price", the sentiments expressed have nothing to do with cowardice or selfishness. Running away from the fighting is never once contemplated as a possibility (the only exception being the farmer Detering, whose mind snaps when he catches sight of some cherry blossom which swamps him with recollections of his home). Life seems all the more precious when death is so close, but this does not cause them to falter when the call comes to attack the enemy. They fight like dangerous animals, but their adversary is not the French or the British—it is death itself, the negation of the life force:

> We are not hurling grenades against people, we are oblivious of all that at this moment, for there is Death in full cry against us.

This existence on the border of death causes them to concern themselves only with the basic essentials; and this is why the episodes of happiness we discussed earlier all concerned the basic physical needs of the comrades: food, defecation, sleep.

CHAPTER 3

All Quiet in Cultural Context

An Interview with Erich Maria Remarque: How Writing *All Quiet* Changed My Life

Frédéric Lefèvre

Much to the dismay of scholars today and during Remarque's lifetime, he was extremely protective of his personal life. Despite living in a fairly high-profile manner, socializing and nightclubbing with celebrities, he rarely talked to the press. At the time the following selection was written, he had been famous for little more than a year, but he was already reclusive and did not grant interviews. In 1930, however, he did talk with a former colleague, French editor Frédéric Lefèvre. The Parisian literary weekly *Nouvelles Littéraires* published the resulting article, which was translated into English and published in a shortened version in a monthly British magazine called *The Living Age*. The interview is casual, with Lefèvre, Remarque, and a friend discussing a variety of topics. The translation is rather stilted by today's standards, but the article gives the flavor of the conversation and the relationships between the men. In the course of the discussion, Remarque comments on why he wrote *All Quiet* and what the resulting fame has meant to him.

Erich Maria Remarque, author of *All Quiet on the Western Front*, has never given an interview and never will give one. He has, however, repeated several times in a way that honors me and fills me with confusion that if he ever breaks his self-imposed rule it will be in my favor, but I do not believe that day will ever come.

Remarque loves France and Paris and he visits our country from time to time. Since he is my friend we see each other and

Reprinted from Frédéric Lefèvre, "An Hour with Erich Remarque," *The Living Age*, December 1930.

converse together at length. In speaking to me, however, he regards me as a friend and not as the editor in chief of the *Nouvelles Littéraires*, so that if I write down word for word one of our most recent conversations I am perhaps betraying his friendship and probably laying myself open to his vehement reproaches. But I am sure, in any event, that I am not betraying his thought. Moreover, I believe it a duty at the present hour, which is so serious for all of Europe, to bring forward a decisive piece of testimony in the cause of peace and international understanding by repeating some of the noble declarations made by an author who to-day possesses the greatest audience in the entire world.

One day, not long ago, Remarque was engaged in a very animated conversation with our mutual friend, Friedrich Hirth, who was about to publish a book entitled *Hitler, or The Unchained Warrior*. These two Germans, Remarque and Hirth, were discussing that great apostle of Franco-German *rapprochement*, Heinrich Heine, whose works Hirth has edited. When I entered, Hirth exclaimed, 'Ah, here is Frédéric Lefèvre. He is the man who ought to give us an impartial, living biography of Heine by way of just reparation to a great poet who has fallen victim to the injustices and inaccuracies of Camille Mauclair.'

'Never mind Camille Mauclair,' I replied. 'Subjects of a more palpitating interest solicit our attention. On the day when Hirth, the political historian, publishes his work on Hitler, I should like his friend Remarque, who has just arrived from Germany, to express a contrasting opinion on this strange character.'

No Politics

'You're on the wrong track, Lefèvre,' said Remarque. 'I have no opinion of Hitler. I know nothing about him. I never occupy myself with political questions. Through honesty. For I believe that politics is such a vast, complicated, and difficult domain that one has to be a politician alone to start adventuring in that direction. For my part, I am trying to be only a writer. Furthermore, I believe that a man who loves justice above all things cannot be a politician, since politics is chiefly a question of forces and equilibrium of forces. A man who loves justice cannot occupy himself with politics because from his first step in this direction he encounters injustice.'

'However,' I replied, 'you have noticed the anxiety that is now tormenting certain modern French writers, even some of those, who, the minute the Armistice was signed, stretched out their hands without *arrière-pensées* [after-thought] in friendship to the writers of Germany. What reply are you going to make to this state of anxiety?'

Remarque reflected a few minutes, looked at me with his handsome blue eyes that have such a loyal flame in them, then glanced at Hirth and said,—

'My dear Lefèvre, I can only say one thing to you, but I believe it profoundly. I am convinced in my soul and conscience that no one in Germany desires war.' He stopped and took thought as if he felt he had not entirely convinced me. 'No desire for war really exists in the soul of the German people.'

'Your statement touches me,' I replied, 'because it is above suspicion. Frenchmen, all of whom have read *All Quiet on the Western Front*, know how fully they can trust the judgment that you are now passing on the German people. But tell us of the circumstances that surrounded the birth of your splendid book.'

'Lefèvre, you irritate me in always wanting to consider me as a writer. I am a man and your friend, that is all, just as I am Hirth's friend. We sympathize as men and not because I wrote *All Quiet on the Western Front* and because you are editor in chief of the *Nouvelles Littéraires*. I am getting tired of telling you that I cannot believe that I have a literary vocation. If I wrote a book, it was done solely because I wanted to discuss seriously with myself a problem that touches me personally. I am a thoroughly normal man.' Here Remarque smiled and looked at Hirth. 'Is the word "normal," my dear friend, the one I should use? I am normal as millions of other men are normal. Furthermore, I believe that the problem that occupies me also occupies millions of other men who are also debating it. I do not care to know whether the book I wrote is interesting or not. I only ask it to give me my own personal solution.'

'And what,' I inquired, 'is the central problem that underlies *All Quiet on the Western Front?*'

COMRADESHIP

'I never had any intention of writing a war book. The very eve of the day I started to write I was not dreaming of any such thing. And then the next morning it was raining. I could not go out. I remained indoors, reflecting, asking why, in spite of the fact that my health was good, my material life well assured, and everything going satisfactorily, I was nevertheless unhappy. I had the impression of being shut off, separated, amputated from some mystery I cannot define. Why was I alone, alone? I don't know how long I kept asking myself why I was in this condition.

'I slowly sought back in my mind, and my memory led me to the time of the War and I realized that during the War I was not alone, I had comrades. Yet of all the comrades I loved during the War none had the same spirit, the same culture as I, yet they were my comrades and I loved them. I had the feeling of being profoundly attached to these men and this feeling did not rest in any way on intellectual values shared in common. And then, as I reflected on the comradeship created by the War, on that communion of spirit that is not based on intellectuality, I came to the conviction that if I should meet the two or three comrades of that period who have survived I should still feel as close to them as during the carnage, whereas nothing could attach me to them if I were to meet them for the first time to-day.

'When all that became clearly fixed in my mind I wanted to probe still deeper by writing. Therefore, it was not inspiration that came to me, for I do not believe in literary inspiration. If I was able to think back with a certain tenderness on what my life had been during the War, explain it by the fact that I was only seventeen and a half when I was mobilized. What a moving age! What does one think about at seventeen? One is beginning to read and beginning to discover music. For my part, I was dreaming that I should become a composer, and behold, I found myself thrown into barracks and then, a few weeks later, I was sent to the front. All my life had changed the moment when I began to organize it freely in accordance with my dreams. And then, suddenly, no more books, no more music, no more spiritual evasions. The roar of cannon and the groans of men in anguish. I became filled with the idea that the course of my life had been profoundly changed and that my development was going to follow a direction different from what I had dreamed.

PATRIOTISM AND DEATH

'At that time I was brimming over with enthusiasm and animated, as all young Germans were, by a great feeling of patriotism. We were all convinced, all we kids of seventeen, that we were fighting for the salvation of the world and the salvation of civilization. I am now quite convinced that young Englishmen and young Frenchmen thought the same thing. But afterward, afterward! The War was too terrible and too long for me not to learn to think otherwise. After it was over I saw all its hideousness, but there was one thing I could not accept.

'I saw my best friend lying in the mud, his abdomen torn open. That is what was really insupportable and incomprehensible, and what is no less incomprehensible is that it required so many post-war years and so much reflection for me to realize the full atrocity of these occurrences. At the time of the fighting, I was struggling between two sentiments that I considered equally intangible. War appealed to me as a necessity for saving culture; but, on the other hand, I thought that nothing was worth the death of so many million men. It was this latter conviction that carried the day and I still hold to it.

'If, from time to time, certain people in Germany accuse me of treason, it is because it is difficult to admit that one can love one's country and at the same time believe that war is not an excellent means of assuring human progress.'

'My dear Lefèvre,' Hirth broke in, 'to understand Remarque fully, remember that he was born in Osnabrück, Westphalia, and that Westphalia . . .'

Remarque interrupted him with a smile.

'Yes, my dear Hirth, I know what you are going to say. Westphalia is populated by peaceful creatures, ponderous, well balanced, who reflect about everything they do and who have wisely arrived at the conviction that one can love all humanity and work with all one's strength for reciprocal understanding among nations, yet love one's own nation above all others.'

NO NEED FOR CRITICS

Remarque offered us some Egyptian cigarettes and I offered him some French cigarettes. He hesitated.

'People tell me that they are too strong,' he said; 'unfortunately, I must look out for my health. You know that I spend six months of the year at Davos in Switzerland because of my lungs. I took refuge in Davos when the success of *All Quiet* began to affirm itself. It was a success which surprised me at the time and which utterly surprises me still, not because I am modest but simply because I feel that I have never written a book. I had hardly arrived at Davos when my publisher wrote me that he was collecting all the criticisms that had appeared and that he was going to forward them to me. I at once asked him to do nothing of the kind. There will always be time, won't there,' said our friend with a smile, 'to go over them when I am fifty years old? I was afraid that if I read them at the beginning of my career they would make me proud or uncertain, and that in either case they would throw me off my track.

'I have never read a single criticism of my book, any more than I have ever granted a single interview. I am unable to understand why people keep wanting to get statements from me, since the best revelation of my soul is in my book, that book which, as far as I am concerned, has but one advantage —that it made me independent. For the rest it does me nothing but harm and by no means the least damage was that it deprived me of friendships that I cherished, especially youthful friendships.

THE PAIN OF FAME

'What actually happened? Before my "success" my friends used to greet me joyfully, but now if I announce that I am going to visit them I no longer find myself in the cordial intimacy of long ago—they receive me flanked with a group of unknown people to whom I seem like some curious animal. All the time, I keep asking myself bitterly whenever someone approaches me, Is he doing this out of sympathy for my own person, or is he so dazzled by my external success that he only wants to boast of having met a "celebrated" man? Formerly when I returned from a six months' journey, all my friends were glad and gave me a party. To-day their susceptibility has no bounds and if I neglect to write one or another of them, he treats me contemptuously. I swear to you, Lefèvre, that my position has become more difficult and more disagreeable than it was before.'

'Have you visited the German Embassy?' Hirth inquired.

Here Remarque assumed such a disgusted expression that all three of us laughed.

'Why do that?' he asked. 'Would they receive me if I had not made this success in which I myself count for nothing? I have but one desire and because you two understand it I see both of you with pleasure. It is that all who come to me forget that I have written a book and speak to me like a man.'

POST-WAR BOOK

'You always say a book, your book,' I pointed out, 'but you have just written another. Did you write it as quickly as the first, which you told us the other day you had entirely finished in the space of six weeks?'

'No, it took much longer than that. I wanted to study how the men who came out of the trenches adapted themselves to post-war conditions. It was necessary to portray them living through an epoch of complete dissolution. Although the action of my new novel takes place in Germany I am persuaded it is common to all nations that fought.'

'What is its title?' I inquired.

'In French it will be *Après*. In German, I have not yet decided.'

'Why is that?'

'I had, of course, fixed upon a title in my mind, *Der Weg Zurück* (*The Way Back*), but I find that another writer has already used it for a book that I know nothing about.'

'It can't be said that no one will see your book, since it will begin appearing a month hence on the same day by installments in all the capitals throughout the world. One great newspaper in each of these capitals has acquired exclusive rights.'

'The composition of my new book was rather difficult. I conceived of a work three times as long as *All Quiet on the Western Front,* but on my own initiative I cut down the manuscript about two-thirds, which makes it only a little longer than my first book. If I have made certain excisions, it was simply not to fatigue the reader with episodes that are almost exactly alike. In principle, all the events I wanted to describe, all post-war events, were similar. So that it was simply a question of choosing the most striking episodes. But enough. Let us pass on to something else. I have never talked so much about my books. If I liked to discuss them I should be nothing but a booster.

"WE LIVE"

'When I have finished my life work I shall be able to ask if what I have done was well done. For the moment I know but one thing, that there are a lot of things left for me to learn and that I am spending my time learning them. I want to read and read a lot. Music fills me with passion and I am fanatically fond of Beethoven. Here is the whole thing in a nutshell. Success, which has no importance and proves nothing, upset my life from top to bottom. I must now bring back order into my life. I thought I should have a slow, progressive success and made my plans accordingly. But look!'

This time I asked, 'Are you, at last, going to stay longer in Paris?'

'Hardly a week, alas. Paris is the part of France I know least well. Last year I toured through your country with a joy that grew from day to day. Normandy, Brittany, Limoges, the Pyrenees, a 3,750-mile automobile trip. What struck me and moved me most in France was the contact I established with the common people, with the simplest and humblest citizens.

'There is a surprising ancient culture throughout all of France, a perfume of antique civilization. If you ask the way of some old peasant his reply is amiable, flowery, cultivated. When I went to some little barber I had the impression that all his answers to my questions showed quickness of mind. Perhaps it has something to do with the language or perhaps it is some emanation of old Latin civilization. In Paris I adore walking in the afternoon when a bluish mist lies over the *quais*, and when I am fatigued I sit down on the terraces of the cafés and look about me.'

'In which respect,' remarked Hirth, 'you resemble Stresemann, who also liked to sit on the terraces of Paris cafés and look at the moving crowd.'

'Yes, for that crowd is life, and I adore life above everything else. Even a book interests me if only it makes us love life better, if it lifts us out of our routine by making us reflect on the greatest of all problems, on the most marvelous of all miracles: we live.'

All Quiet Is False and Seditious

Compiled by C.R. Owen

Although *All Quiet on the Western Front* became an international bestseller, even in Germany, the novel raised the ire of many people. Most of the anger came from German Nationalists who felt that Remarque's novel showed Germany, German soldiers, and war in a bad light. These Nationalists were already looking forward to the day when Germany would be at war again, and they knew it was important to keep the citizenry focused on German military pride, not an easy task after the defeat of World War I. In contrast to the proud German ideal, Remarque's soldiers were mostly young, green, and naïve, and, although they did feel that they were serving their country, they also acknowledged the futility and absurdity of war and of the people who commanded them. The few officers in the novel tended to be shown as cruel martinets. All in all, Remarque had painted a far from flattering and glorious portrait of German soldiery.

Remarque's German critics went to great lengths to discredit not only the novel but Remarque himself, often making up lies about him. These critiques are, for the most part, not available in English, but scholar C.R. Owen compiled a massive, extremely detailed bibliography of all the things that had been written about Remarque up until 1984. The bibliography contained paraphrases and quotations from most of the writings, including several of the critical comments about *All Quiet.* This selection is excerpted from Owen's compilation of adverse criticisms of *All Quiet.* Owen's comments are in italics. The critics' remarks are in plain type.

Anonymous, Munich, October 20, 1929: "The characteristic of German par excellence, their heroism since the time of the Goths and the Langobards immortalized in the battle of Teu-

Reprinted from C.R. Owen, *Erich Maria Remarque: A Critical Bio-Bibliography* (Amsterdam: Rodopi, 1984), by permission of the publisher.

toburg, the War of Liberation and the World War, which are among the most beautiful monuments of German heroism, are being ruined by the Jewish culture-destroyers and the Bolshevists . . . like Toller and Remarque, whose pamphlet (sic) *All Quiet* . . . is full of contempt for the front-soldier and destroys his heroism and bravery. . . ."

UNTRUE PORTRAYAL

Eugen von Frauenholz quite correctly states that every soldier probably has a different experience in and recollection of the war and that hence no one account of it can do it justice. And furthermore that "the core of our nation was healthy, otherwise the army could not have accomplished such brilliant tasks, nor could the nation have withstood the incredible pressure for four-and-a-half years. And therefore, the old front-line soldier rejects books like *All Quiet* . . . and similar products . . . simply because they are untrue. . . ."

SPIRIT OF DEFEAT

Georg Friedrich Jünger writes . . . "The success of a book like the novel *All Quiet* . . . would be incomprehensible if one were to ignore the political situation of Germany at the time of its appearance. This book expresses best the spirit of defeat. A private citizen without any patriotism and without a national awareness, condemns war because it smashed, crudely and without consideration, into the most private enjoyments of this bourgeois youth, imposing duties on him which he performed, not voluntarily, but by compulsion and with repugnance. Such a book that does not portray the heroic battles of the German armies but engages in the weakly complaints against war does not only gladden the hearts of the pacifists, it simultaneously supplies a weapon to the champions of tributary policies who proclaim it an Homeric work of art, and who play it off against the pioneers of the political war of liberation. It gave rise to a clear-cut division of attitudes and made possible the survey of political power-groupings, which was not without value. . . ."

FALSE DEPICTION

Gottfried [Nickl's] contribution, not only to the Remarque-diatribe, but to basic Fascist ideology, must be the ultimate in perversion; it quite seriously claims that war is true peace, the army and the soldiery the true aspirants and defenders of pacifism. . . .

[Nickl's] actual Remarque diatribe begins on p. 20 [of his

A FORGOTTEN BOOK

Although most of the criticism came from the Nationalists who felt the novel undermined the German military image, Remarque also received criticism from the Left, many of whom liked the novel, but disliked his lack of commitment to its message. One of his early German Leftist critics was Carl von Ossietzky, a patriotic German commentator who wanted to see his country tread the path to peace, not another war. Ossietzky was actively anti-Nazi and was outspoken in his writings. In the early 1930s he was imprisoned for extended periods for his views, and in 1935 he received the Nobel Peace Prize while still in prison. In 1938, he died of tuberculosis while still a prisoner. The following excerpt is taken from a 1932 essay, "The Remarque Case."

Nobody will ever be able to puzzle out how it came about that Erich Maria Remarque became a sort of model ogre in the propaganda of the right. His war novel is certainly a great achievement, filled with very realistic detail; but it lacks what is needed; to go beyond that and become a fact. Even without "tendency" laid on with a trowel, a novel dealing with the strongest experience of a generation has to be effective beyond literature, in the field of the political. This did not happen in this case, and the book remains simply an interesting isolated achievement. Its enormous sale has done no harm to nationalism. Basically this book has passed by without effect. It was accepted as the fashionable book, read as such, and then put away. . . .

His book is already forgotten. The author would be forgotten too, did revengeful fury of the chauvinists not repeatedly remind us of him. Why is such hatred directed against the author of "All Quiet on the Western Front"? It is scarcely possible to answer this question. Perhaps those on the other side feel what a sharp weapon this book could have become had there been a man behind it. But this man is lacking; only a child of fortune who happened to hit the jackpot, and thereupon immediately retired into private life.

forty-four page critique]: "it is clear that he who proclaims war as a senseless horror is unable to praise the men who, with the weapons in their hands, the heroes, are the examples of mankind." *[Nickl] takes exception to Remarque's description of: a lack of heroism among the soldiers; the description of the officers (characterized by Himmelstoss and the officer Bäumer meets on the street when on furlough at*

*home); the difference between the officers and the enlisted
men, their food, supplies, comforts etc.; he equally objects to
the description of the medics and doctors as being sadistic in
their entirety, the hospitals, the care of the wounded, the
prayers, even to the differences in the brothels! He rejects Remarque's treatment of the soldier's concern with food and
defecation and the language employed, including such words
as eating (fressen) and "shitting," these words not being common to soldiers! [Nickl states that] Remarque's description of
the "heroic" attack at Langemark is not to be equated with
the truth of this heroic encounter, nor with the demand by
Frederick the Great, when he addressed his cadets: "Let him
die decently."*

*The entire descriptive aspect of the novel is one-sided, [says
Nickl,] only those "who were destroyed by the war, even if they escaped the grenades" were shown, unlike Jüngers In Stahlgewittern (In Storms of Steel) and others.* "Remarque basically depicts
no more than a number of uprooted young people who were
emotionally unstable even before going to war and who experienced the war internally. But this group is not representative of
the bulk of German youths and their magnificent record in
war—nor is it proper to speak of 'an entire generation that was
destroyed. . . .' Remarque's narrative is amply compared to that
of Jünger, who is the true representative of humanity. In conclusion, a few loose ends are tied up. War is interpreted to be the
brazen, inexorable law of nature which man can not alter one
whit. The various characters are designed to slight Germany
and the national honor: Katczinski, a mere Pole, is shown to ex-
cel over all the "poorly trained, unknowledgeable Germans"; *the
French girls and the Russian prisoners are described with great
empathy, nothing is being said about the Germans. The act of
killing the French soldier and the subsequent confession of guilt is
pure trivia: why did he kill the French soldier? If that is the way
Bäumer felt, why did he not take him prisoner, which would have
been the simplest thing in the world. . . .*

*Dr. Gottfried Nickl was an early member of the Nazi Party
in Austria and through the efficient distribution-organization
of it, this pamphlet reached the record figure of 200,000 by
January of 1930. . . .*

PROMOTES DANGEROUS PACIFISM

*Graf von Schlieffen's review deals less with the literary aspects
of the novel than with its sociological implications: In a*

*clever way Remarque is said to compose all that which ap-
pears repulsive in war, trying to elicit the thought: "No war
ever again" in his reader.* "Beautiful and elevating experiences are totally missing. . . . This book, precisely because it
is so seemingly harmless will, in its mass distribution in
Germany, contribute in impressive ways to the promotion of
a pacifist attitude. Its main danger lies in that the readers do
not even notice this tendency."

The Year I Learned to Love a German

Mordecai Richler

Canadian novelist Mordecai Richler was a puny, unathletic, book-loving Jewish teenager in 1944. Like most people in the Allied nations, he had lived through several years of anti-German propaganda and had read about the atrocities committed by the Germans. In the black-and-white terms of many teenagers, Richler hated Germans.

Then one day, out of boredom, he reluctantly picked up *All Quiet on the Western Front.* Within a few pages he was captivated. In this selection, he tells how that book allowed him to see for the first time that Germans could not be lumped together as monsters. The book vividly showed him that there was little difference between the ordinary German soldier and the ordinary Canadian, American, or French soldier. All of them suffered horrors of war; all of them were people, some good, some bad, fulfilling their responsibility to their country at the cost of their own innocence.

Reading was not one of my boyhood passions. Girls, or rather the absence of girls, drove me to it. When I was 13 years old, short for my age, more than somewhat pimply, I was terrified of girls. They made me feel sadly inadequate. As far as I could make out, they were attracted only to boys who were tall or played for the school basketball team or at least shaved. Unable to qualify on all three counts, I resorted to subterfuge. I set out to call attention to myself by becoming a character. Retreating into high seriousness, I acquired a pipe, which I chewed on ostentatiously, and made it my business to be seen everywhere, even at school basketball games, absorbed by books of daunting significance. Say, H.G. Wells's "Short History of the World" or Paul de Kruif's

Reprinted from Mordecai Richler, "1944: The Year I Learned to Love a German," *The New York Times*, Book Review, February 2, 1986, by permission of the author.

"Microbe Hunters" or John Gunther inside one continent or another. I rented these thought-provoking books for three cents a day from a neighborhood lending library that was across the street from a bowling alley where I used to spot pins four nights a week.

Oh, my God, I would not be 13 again for anything. The sweetly scented girls of my dreams, wearing lipstick and tight sweaters and nylon stockings, would sail into the bowling alley holding hands with the boys from the basketball team. "Hi," they would call out, giggly, nudging one another, even as I bent over the pins, "how goes the reading?"

The two women who ran the lending library, possibly amused by my pretensions, tried to interest me in fiction.

"I Can't Be Bothered with *Stories*"

"I want fact. I can't be bothered with *stories*," I protested, waving my pipe at them, affronted. "I just haven't got the time for such nonsense."

I knew what novels were, of course. I had read "Scaramouche," by Rafael Sabatini, at school, as well as "Treasure Island" and some Ellery Queens and a couple of thumpers by G.A. Henty. Before that there had been Action Comics, Captain Marvel, Batman and—for educational reasons—either Bible Comics or Classic Comics. All these treasures I bought under the counter, as it were. They were passed hand to hand on dark street corners. Contraband. Our samizdat. The reason for this being that in 1943 the dolts who prevailed in Ottawa [the seat of the government] had adjudged American comic books unessential to the war effort, a drain on the Canadian dollar.

Novels, I knew, were mere romantic make-believe, not as bad as poetry, to be fair, but bad enough. Our high school class master, a dedicated Scot, had been foolish enough to try to interest us in poetry. A veteran of World War I, he told us that during the nightly bombardments on the Somme he would fix a candle to his steel helmet so that he could read poetry in the trenches. A scruffy lot, we were not moved. Instead we exchanged knowing winks behind that admirable man's back. Small wonder, we agreed, that he had ended up no better than a high school teacher.

My aunts consumed historical novels like pastries. My father read Black Mask and True Detective. My mother would read anything on a Jewish subject, preferably by I.J. Singer or

Sholem Asch, though she would never forgive the latter for having written "The Nazarene," never mind "Mary" and "The Apostle." My older brother kept a novel, "Topper Takes a Trip," secure under his mattress in the bedroom we shared, assuring me that it was placed at just such an angle on the springs that if it were moved so much as a millimeter in his absence he would know and bloody well make me pay for it.

I fell ill with a childhood disease, I no longer remember which, but obviously I meant it as a rebuke to those girls in tight sweaters who continued to ignore me. Never mind, they would mourn at my funeral, burying me with my pipe. Too late, they would say, "Boy, was he ever an intellectual!"

The women from the lending library, concerned, dropped off books for me at our house. The real stuff. Fact-filled. Providing me with the inside dope on Theodor Herzl's childhood and "Brazil Yesterday, Today, and Tomorrow." One day they brought me a novel: "All Quiet on the Western Front" by Erich Maria Remarque. The painting on the jacket that was taped to the book showed a soldier wearing what was unmistakably a German Army helmet. *What was this,* I wondered, *some sort of bad joke?*

"I WISHED EVERY GERMAN DEATH"

Nineteen forty-four that was, and I devoutly wished every German left on the face of the earth an excruciating death. The Allied invasion of France had not yet begun, but I cheered every Russian counterattack, each German city bombed, and—with the help of a map tacked to my bedroom wall—followed the progress of the Canadian troops fighting their way up the Italian boot. Boys from our street had already been among the fallen. Izzy Draper's uncle. Harvey Kugelmass's older brother. The boy who was supposed to marry Gita Holtzman.

"All Quiet on the Western Front" lay unopened on my bed for two days. A time bomb ticking away, though I hardly suspected it. Rather than read a novel, a novel written by a German, I tuned in to radio soap operas in the afternoons: "Ma Perkins," "Pepper Young's Family." I organized a new baseball league for short players who didn't shave yet, appointing myself commissioner, the first Canadian to be so honored. Sifting through a stack of my father's back issues of *Popular Mechanics,* I was sufficiently inspired to invent a spaceship and fly to Mars, where I was adored by everybody, especially the girls. Finally, I was driven to picking up "All Quiet on the Western Front" out of boredom. I never expected that a mere novel, a stranger's tale, could actually be dangerous, creating such turbulence in my life, obliging me to question so many received ideas. About Germans. About my own monumental ignorance of the world. About what novels were.

At the age of 13 in 1944, happily as yet untainted by English 104, I couldn't tell you whether Remarque's novel was a. a slice of life b. symbolic c. psychological d. seminal.

MY SEDUCTION

I couldn't even say if it was well or badly written. In fact, as I recall, it didn't seem to be "written" at all. Instead, it just flowed. Now, of course, I understand that writing that doesn't advertise itself is art of a very high order. It doesn't come easily. But at the time I wasn't capable of making such distinctions. I also had no notion of how "All Quiet on the Western Front" rated critically as a war novel. I hadn't read [the great war novels by] Stendhal or Tolstoy or Crane or Hemingway. I hadn't even heard of them. I didn't know that Thomas Mann, whoever he was, had praised the novel highly. Neither did I know that in 1929 the judges at some outfit called the Book-of-the-Month Club had made it their May selection. But what I did know is that, hating Germans with a passion, I had read only 20, maybe 30, pages before the author had seduced me into identifying with my enemy, 19-year-old Paul Bäumer, thrust into the bloody trenches of World War I with his schoolmates: Müller, Kemmerich and the reluctant Joseph Behm, one of the first to fall. As if that weren't sufficiently unsettling in itself, the author, having won my love for Paul, my enormous concern for his survival, then betrayed me in the last dreadful paragraphs of his book:

"He fell in October 1918, on a day that was so quiet and still on the whole front, that the army report confined itself to the single sentence: All quiet on the Western Front.

"He had fallen forward and lay on the earth as though sleeping. Turning him over one saw that he could not have suffered long; his face had an expression of calm, as though almost glad the end had come."

The movies, I knew from experience, never risked letting you down like that. No matter how bloody the battle, how long the odds, Errol Flynn, Robert Taylor, even Humphrey

SENTIMENTAL RESTRAINT
L. Kronenberger reviewed All Quiet *for the* New York
Times *on June 2, 1929.*

There is one further quality about "All Quiet" in addition to its
magnificent physical picture of war and its burden of a lost
generation, and that is its humanity. It is an objective book, an
ironic book, but it is never callous, never hard-boiled, never
unfeeling. There is almost no stock pathos, but there is a
warmth, a youthful sadness, a release of natural emotions un-
burdened by that sentimental restraint common to the men in
[the war novel] "Journey's End."

Bogart could be counted on to survive and come home to
Ann Sheridan, Lana Turner or—if they were sensitive types—
Loretta Young. Only character actors, usually Brooklyn
Dodgers fans, say George Tobias or William Bendix, were
expendable.

Obviously, having waded into the pool of serious fiction
by accident, I was not sure I liked or trusted the water. It was
too deep. Anything could happen.

There was something else, a minor incident in "All Quiet
on the Western Front" that would not have troubled an adult
reader but, I'm embarrassed to say, certainly distressed that
13-year-old boy colliding with his first serious novel.

Sent out to guard a village that has been abandoned because it is being shelled too heavily, Katczinsky, the incom-
parable scrounger, surfaces with suckling pigs and potatoes
and carrots for his comrades, a group of eight altogether:

"The suckling pigs are slaughtered. Kat sees to them. We
want to make potato-cakes to go with the roast. But we cannot find a grater for the potatoes. However, that difficulty is
soon got over. With a nail we punched a lot of holes in a pot
lid and there we have a grater. Three fellows put on thick
gloves to protect their fingers against the grater, two others
peel the potatoes, and the business gets going."

The business, I realized, alarmed—no, *affronted*—was the
making of potato latkes, a favorite of mine as well as Paul
Bäumer's, a dish I had always taken to be Jewish, certainly
not a German concoction.

What did I know? Nothing. Or, looked at another way, my
real education, my lifelong addiction to fiction, began with
the trifling discovery that the potato latke was not of Jewish

origin, but something borrowed from the Germans and now a taste that Jew and German shared in spite of everything.

NOVELS ARE DANGEROUS

I felt easier about my affection for the German soldier Paul Bäumer once I was told by the women from the lending library that when Hitler came to power in 1933 he had burned all of Erich Maria Remarque's books and in 1938 he took away his German citizenship. Obviously Hitler had grasped that novels could be dangerous, something I learned when I was only 13 years old. He burned them, I began to devour them. I started to read at the breakfast table and on streetcars, often missing my stop, and in bed with benefit of a flashlight. It got me into trouble. I grasped, for the first time, that I didn't live in the center of the world but had been born into a working-class family in an unimportant country far from the cities of light: London, Paris, New York. Of course this wasn't my fault, it was my inconsiderate parents who were to blame. But there was, I now realized, a larger world out there beyond St. Urbain Street in Montreal; a world that could be available to me, even though—to my mother's despair—I had been born left-handed, ate with my elbows on the table and had failed once more to lead the class at school.

Preparing myself for the *Rive Gauche*, I bought a blue beret, but I didn't dare wear it outside, or even in the house if anybody else was at home. I looked at but lacked the courage to buy a cigarette holder. But the next time I took Goldie Zimmerman to a downtown movie and then out to Dinty Moore's for toasted tomato sandwiches, I suggested that instead of milkshakes we each order a glass of *vin ordinaire*. "Are you crazy?" she asked.

As my parents bickered at the supper table, trapped in concerns now far too mundane for the likes of me—what to do if Dworkin raised the rent again, how to manage my brother's college fees—I sat with but actually apart from them in the kitchen, enthralled, reading for the first time, "All happy families are alike but an unhappy family is unhappy after its own fashion."

THE AUTHOR

Erich Maria Remarque, born in Westphalia in 1897, went off to war, directly from school, at the age of 18. He was wounded five times. He lost all his friends. After the war he worked briefly as a schoolteacher, a stonecutter, a test driver for a tire company and an editor of *Sportbild* magazine. His first novel, "Im Westen Nichts Neues," was turned down by several publishers before it was brought out by the Ullstein Press in Berlin in 1928. "All Quiet on the Western Front" sold 1,200,000 copies in Germany and was translated into 29 languages, selling some four million copies throughout the world. The novel has been filmed three times; the first, memorably, by Lewis Milestone in 1930. The Milestone version, with Lew Ayres playing Paul Bäumer, won Academy Awards for best picture and best direction.

Since "All Quiet on the Western Front" once meant so much to me, I picked it up again with a certain anxiety. After all this time I find it difficult to be objective about the novel. Its pages still evoke for me a back bedroom with a cracked ceiling and a sizzling radiator on St. Urbain Street, mice scrabbling in the walls, a window looking out on sheets frozen stiff on the laundry line, and all the pain of being too young to shave, an ignorant and bewildered boy of 13.

Over the years the novel has lost something in shock value. The original jacket copy of the 1929 Little, Brown & Company edition of "All Quiet on the Western Front" warns the reader that it is "at times crude" and "will shock the supersensitive by its outspokeness." Contemporary readers, far from being shocked, will be amused by the novel's discretion, the absence of explicit sex scenes, the unbelievably polite dialogue of the men in the trenches.

A NOVEL THAT WILL ENDURE

The novel also has its poignant moments, both in the trenches and when Paul Bäumer goes home on leave, an old man of 19, only to find insufferably pompous schoolmasters still recruiting the young with mindless prattle about the fatherland and the glory of battle. Strong characters are deftly sketched. Himmelstoss, the postman who becomes a crazed drillmaster. Tjaden, the peasant soldier. Kantorek, the schoolmaster. On the front line the enemy is never the Frogs or the Limeys, but the insanity of the war itself. It is the war, in fact, and not even Paul Bäumer, that is the novel's true protagonist. In a brief introduction to the novel Remarque wrote: "This book is to be neither an accusation nor a confession, and least of all an adventure, for death is not an adventure to those who stand face to face with it. It will try simply to tell of a generation of men who, even though they may have escaped its shells, were destroyed by the war."

Since World War I we have become altogether too familiar with larger horrors. The Holocaust, Hiroshima, the threat of a nuclear winter. Death by numbers, cities obliterated by decree. At peace, as it were, we live with the daily dread of the missiles in their silos, ours pointed at them, theirs pointed at us. None of this, however, diminishes the power of "All Quiet on the Western Front," a novel that will endure because of its humanity, its honor and its refusal to lapse into sentimentality or strike a false note. It is a work that has earned its place on that small shelf of World War I classics alongside "Goodbye to All That," by Robert Graves, and Ernest Hemingway's "A Farewell to Arms."

A Debate on the Bowdlerization of *All Quiet on the Western Front*

Canadian Forum

All Quiet on the Western Front was published in Germany in early 1929. Shortly after, it was translated into English and published in both England and the United States. The U.S. publication, however, was clouded by scandal. The book was to be distributed by the Book-of-the-Month Club—a boon to any author because club selections routinely sold millions of copies. In this instance, however, BOMC executives insisted that certain parts of the novel were too racy for American readers and must be expurgated before they would distribute the book. The cuts were small, but they aroused the ire of writers and the general public. Censorship should not be allowed to occur in the United States, the land of the free.

Despite First Amendment protection, however, the U.S. had a history of banning or censoring books containing frank sexual depictions and language. D.H. Lawrence's *Lady Chatterly's Lover* and James Joyce's *Ulysses*, for example, were two of the many victims of U.S. censorship and were not legally available in the U.S. for many decades. Americans, it seemed, could not distinguish between pornography and meritorious works containing sexual scenes. (The debate on this issue still shows up in American courts from time to time.) Books deemed pornographic were not only not available in stores, but could not be sent through the mails without risk of severe penalty.

BOMC executives claimed to be worried that if they left *All Quiet* intact, they would be subject to federal penalties. The viewpoint below is made up of three short selections—

Reprinted from *The Canadian Forum*, Letters to the Editor, August, September, and November 1929.

an essay by an anonymous Canadian journalist (it was the editorial fashion for much of this century for magazine columnists to be unnamed, not out of fear of reprisal, but more likely because the columnists represented not just themselves but the publication as a whole) condemning the BOMC's action; a response by a BOMC executive; and a comment by one of the magazine's readers.

When the 'Book of the Month' Club first appeared, no one was inclined to object to it. If a group of the most competent literary minds constituted themselves a committee to select in all the current welter of print one book per month which in their opinion was of outstanding merit, it was not easy to see what harm could come of it. And the good was obvious. Everybody reads, few can choose for themselves. Three cheers for the book clubs!

That is the argument with which most of us began. And, on the whole, the clubs—especially the American Club— have selected well and put notable literature in the hands of their clients. Yet, in spite of this, a certain uneasiness is springing up and promises to assert itself more strongly as the months—the book-months—go by. To take a quite recent instance, the 'Book of the Month' Club selects Remarque's *All Quiet on the Western Front*—a book, by the way, which had already selected itself as one of the most powerful of recent war-books and was in little need of sponsorship. But waiving this minor objection that the Club was flogging a dead horse—or overfeeding a thoroughbred—what do we find? The Club comes to the opinion that the text is here and there unsuited for general circulation and mildly expurgates the American edition, claiming that by so doing they are improving the book and giving it a real advantage over the unexpurgated or less expurgated London edition.

Now, if there is such a thing as vice and virtue in the literary life—I belong to those who answer the implied question in the affirmative—here is an action which is as full of vice as an egg is of meat. The fact that it is performed at the instance of a committee of distinguished men of letters does nothing to palliate the offence, it simply lifts it from the level of the peccadillo to that of high crime.

To begin with, there is the objection that the committee are acting in closer co-operation with the publishing world than is consistent with the healthy exercise of their functions. The only course for such a body of experts is scrupulously to preserve their aloofness from business interests, to choose their book, announce their choice in the current press, and wash their hands of the rest. Circulation should not concern them. Whether their book sells in hundreds, thousands, or millions they should consider their work done the moment their choice is made. If they preserve their strict independence from the commercial dissemination of literature and confine themselves to their proper field—the judging and recommending of books—their work, whatever its value to mankind, is morally irreproachable. But once they open their door to the selling interests, their prestige—to put it mildly—is somewhat shaken.

This is the lesser part of the offence. More serious is the question of expurgation. What business has this group of writers and critics tampering with another man's work (brutally frank, no doubt, but utterly sincere, and acceptable to Europeans)? Is not this the very treatment which they would most bitterly resent if it were dealt out to themselves? And they, who are neither policemen nor censors nor any guardians of the public morality, perpetuate this offence against a fellow-craftsman! And do so in the interest of enlarging the sale of a book!

Granted that they acted with the best of intentions, that they only interfered slightly, almost imperceptibly, with their author's text, that in this particular case, taken quite by itself, no serious harm was done, the fact remains that they have set up a grievous precedent and have put a blot on their escutcheon, which it will be hard for them to remove. Does not the veriest tyro in literature recognize that expurgation is the thin end of the censor's wedge and that censorship is just as foolish and just as dangerous to creative writing as it was in Central Europe a hundred years ago? Are we to condone the practice of censoring and expurgating because it is undertaken by a body of experts? Not at all. If some magistrate or cabinet minister does it, we can at least console ourselves and exonerate him by saying that he was betrayed by his official stupidity. But when a committee of literary men assume his robes and bearing, there is no way out. The offence is rank. It smells to heaven.

There is only side to this question. The censorship is *always* wrong. Theoretically a case can be made for it. If the business of censorship could be entrusted to some profoundly wise and respected person, there might conceivably be moments when he could step in with advantage. The trouble is that there is that in the very nature of censorship which prevents a wise man from meddling with it and either the office must lapse or folly must administer it. The surest proof of the unwisdom of censoring lies in the type of mind that almost invariably undertakes it. If the censorship is not always wrong—I believe that it *is* always wrong—then we can compromise upon the modified statement, equally satisfactory to me and equally efficacious, that it is always wrongly handled.

Consider the present condition of letters. There is under way at this moment one of the strongest and sincerest attempts at frankness that modern literature has seen. Writers like James Joyce, D.H. Lawrence, and Aldous Huxley—to name three leading exponents—prompted by no trivial motives, have gone as far as they could in laying bare the mind and body of man and in insisting that the world must see and learn. Huxley thus far has retained his London publisher but Joyce was long ago driven to Paris and now Lawrence is publishing in Florence. Let me admit freely that Lawrence's latest book, *Lady Chatterly's Lover,* probably exceeds all previous novels in its explicit study of the sexual life. Taking this book alone, the question of its circulating freely is arguable, though I should be in favour of it.

But—and here is the abysmal folly of censorship, exposed as never before—what can it profit to bottle up or prohibit or otherwise interfere with the mental life and influence of an idealist like Lawrence—I am not one of his followers and read him quite inconstantly—when every other movie show, to say nothing of popular literature, is saturated with the worst kind of sexual suggestion. I saw a movie the other day in which, short of performing the sexual act on the screen—I am old-fashioned enough not to approve of this—there was nothing omitted. For any normally intelligent and healthy mind the sexual experience was vividly presented as a barbaric, ruinous, and sweetly desirable consummation. The performance was open to all ages and was received with silent satisfaction. Who in our day has not seen the like? Meanwhile D.H. Lawrence is being driven to publish in holes and corners. That is what I mean when I say that the censorship is always wrong. It hurts the good writer who has no choice but to be frank and it leaves the door wide open for all the smaller insidious fry who know how to put their tongue in their cheeks.

The censorship is always wrong. And now it is confronting us from an unexpected angle.

Inconstant Reader

CHANGES MADE TO AVOID GOVERNMENT CENSORSHIP

The Editor, *The Canadian Forum.*
Sir:

May I ask you to make a slight correction of a statement made in an article printed in your August issue about the Book-of-the-Month Club and Erich Remarque's book, *All Quiet on the Western Front.*

The point of view of the writer is unexceptionable. We in this organization agree with him, and so (I am sure) would our five judges: that they would be far overstepping their function if they ever presumed to act as censors, particularly in the interest of increasing sales. And, in fact, neither in this case, nor in any other, have they so acted. Your contributor was simply misinformed on this point, owing of course to misleading newspaper reports.

The few slight changes that were made by the publishers in the American edition of *All Quiet on the Western Front* were not made at all with the idea of 'improving' the book, or increasing its sales; far from it. Their only object was to make sure that the book could be distributed at all in the United States.

Here is the statement, in part, of the vice-president of the publishing house, Mr. Jenkins, as printed in the *New York Times*, when this accusation of 'censorship' was first brought up:—

> The changes were made for two reasons. First, the book would be sent through the mails, and we did not want to conflict with the Federal laws. Second, inasmuch as it was being published in Boston, we did not want to conflict with the Massachusetts book laws, which have been widely discussed recently and which are exceedingly stringent.
>
> We made the changes entirely on our own responsibility, and have done so in other cases. When we heard that the Book-of-the-Month Club was going to take our book, we made a few additional changes at their suggestion.

The 'few additional changes' they refer to as coming from us were suggested chiefly by William Allen White—out of his editorial experience and for the same reason, to further insure the book's mailability.

If there is anybody or anything to blame for occurrences of this kind, it is the public (in my opinion) which, I suppose, must be in sympathy with federal postal regulations, and such state censorship laws as that of Massachusetts which the publishers are obliged to observe.

The president of Little Brown & Co., Mr. McIntyre, in a candid public statement explained the dilemma in which his firm was placed; he could allow the English translation to remain as it was, with the chance (and it was a very good one) of this great book being banned from the mails altogether; or make a few slight changes, and insure its distribution. Both he and this organization felt that it was wise (under such circumstances) to make the changes.

Yours etc.,
Robert K. Haas,
President, Book-of-the-Month Club, Inc.

TIMIDITY WON THE DAY

The Editor, *The Canadian Forum.*
Sir:

I feel that more needs to be said about the mutilation of Remarque's *All Quiet on the Western Front* by the Book-of-the-Month Club.

Mr. Haas, the president, admits in your September issue that after the publishers thought they had made an honest book of it, further mutilations were carried out on the instructions of one of the five judges of the club 'out of his editorial experience'; with, one may legitimately suppose, the blessing of the other four. This is in itself surely sufficient to justify the charge of mischievous censorship originally made in *The Canadian Forum.*

But the blame! The blame is laid successively on the doorstep of the Federal postal regulations, on that of the unfortunate Book-a-month reading public itself, and finally in a decently swathed form, on the doorstep of Little, Brown & Co., who began the censoring *before* the book was selected by the Club (not we hope with an eye to having it selected).

The dilemma of these five judges is now patent. Either to condone (and connive at) the literary crime of mutilating a work of art, or to run the risk of failing to give the great American public an admirably educative picture of the war. Timidity won the day, and with the aid of the judges the book was made a 'nice' war-story, nice enough to go through the mails. Not that their decision was made with a view to increasing sales. 'Far from it,' says Mr. Haas with emphasis—but only to make sure that it would sell at all.

Now, not only has the cutting obviously impaired the didactic-national value of the book, but the claim to disinterest national service is nonsense, if adduced as the motive for that cutting. The English edition is of course frank, but in no sense and nowhere indecent. And what I object to is Mr. Haas' tacit assumption that the book is obscene, and on the face of it unfit for mailing. The major excision is nothing more offensive than the scene at the latrines in the early part of the book; and the rest follow suit. Now, if the State of Massachusetts or the Federal law, in an excess of coprophobia had been idiotic enough to ban the English translation, the well-known consequence would have been immediate fame and universal consumption of the book; and what could better serve the nationally educative aim of the judges, supposing them to be sincere? What in addition could better have preserved intact whatever degree of reputation for artistic integrity the judges may once have possessed?

There is the case of the lady who wrote to the editor of a certain annual collection of Best Short Stories, indignantly pointing out how poor they were. The reply, indicated in the nature of the case, was that the editor in no way guaranteed that the stories in his compilation were good short stories, but only that they were the best short stories.

Let us avoid indignation lest the Club reply in similar vein that 'The Book-of-the-Month' is not The only book, nor even *The* book that the author wrote.

If I were a citizen of the U.S. I should be seriously indignant, but after all, for us it is a trivial matter. It simply means that a substantial body of Canadians will buy the English in preference to the U.S. edition (however sponsored) of works appearing in the future.

Yours, etc.,
R. MacCallum.

Chronology

1898

Erich Paul Remark born on June 22 in Osnabrück, Germany, to Peter Franz Remark, a bookbinder, and Anna Maria Stallknecht; Spanish-American War.

1900

Germany builds up its sea power; Social Democratic party is established in Russia; United States annexes Hawaii.

1901

Remarque's six-year-old brother, Theo, dies.

1903

Remarque's sister Elfriede is born; World Series begins.

1905

Russian democrats split between moderate Mensheviks and extreme Bolsheviks, presaging revolution; Einstein publishes his theory of relativity.

1907

Second Hague Peace conference; Germany opposes arms limitations.

1909

Henry Ford begins assembly line.

1912

Titanic sinks.

1914

Serbian nationalist assassinates Austria's Archduke Francis Ferdinand, precipitating World War I.

1915–1916

Remarque attends Catholic Teacher's College

1916

November: Remarque is drafted into army.

1917

United States joins war against Germany; Remarque is sent to western front in June and assigned to sapper group; carries friend out of enemy fire; receives serious shrapnel wounds at Battle of Flanders in August and is transferred to St. Vincenz Hospital, Duisburg, German; mother suffers lingering cancer and dies in September.

1918

Poetry first published in avant-garde journal *Die Schönheit*; declared fit for active duty on November 7; German emperor William II abdicates, leaving way for Weimar Republic; World War I ends on November 11; Remarque is discharged and returns to teaching.

1919

Germany signs punishing Versailles treaty; Benito Mussolini founds the Fascist movement in Italy.

1920

Remarque publishes first novel, *Die Traumbude* (*The Dream Room*), and leaves teaching career by end of year; women get the vote in the United States; first Agatha Christie mystery is published.

1922

Remarque works at odd jobs: sells tombstones, plays organ at mental hospital, becomes the publicity director for Continental Rubber Company; adds name Maria to his own; Pharaoh Tutankhamen's tomb is discovered in Egypt.

1923

Adolf Hitler, founder of the National Socialist party, attempts to overthrow Bavarian government but is arrested; begins writing *Mein Kampf* while in jail; George Gershwin's *Rhapsody in Blue* premiers.

1925

Remarque moves to Berlin, center of German publishing; becomes picture editor of *Sport im Bild*, a car-racing magazine; marries divorceé Jutta Ilse Ingeborg Ellen Zambona Winkelhoff on October 14.

1926

Remarque begins using French spelling of his last name, Remarque, on some published writing.

1927

Charles Lindberg makes first transatlantic flight; talking movies begin.

1927–1928

Station am Horizont (*Station on the Horizon*) is serialized in *Sport im Bild*; Remarque begins writing *All Quiet on the Western Front.*

1928

All Quiet is rejected by one publisher but accepted by another (Ullstein) on condition that it first be serialized in *Die Vossische Zeitung*, owned by Ullstein; Walt Disney introduces Mickey Mouse.

1929

All Quiet is published as a hardcover book in Germany and shortly after in Britain and the United States; it is an international best-seller and Remarque becomes famous, although he shuns publicity; some suggest that Remarque's pacifist novel will win him the Nobel Peace Prize, but the German Officer's League responds to the rumor with a letter of protest to the Nobel Prize Committee; "Remarque" becomes official spelling of his last name; stock market collapses and Great Depression begins.

1930

All Quiet is banned in Thuringia, Germany, schools as "pacifist, Marxist propaganda"; Remarque and Jutta divorce (some sources say this occurred in 1929), though they remain friends and housemates; Remarque writes *The Road Back*, as sequel to *All Quiet*; the American film *All Quiet on the Western Front* premieres in December, arousing German protest and riots; the film is banned in Germany.

1931

Remarque buys villa on Lake Maggiore in Porto Ronco, Switzerland; the Irish Free State, in sympathy with Germany and out of antipathy toward Great Britain, bans Remarque's *The Road Back* and six other "anti-German" books.

1932

German government seizes Remarque's German bank funds.

1933

January: Nazis take over German government: Remarque and Jutta flee to Switzerland; Nazis burn books by Remarque and other "traitors"; German president Paul von Hindenburg appoints Adolf Hitler chancellor of Germany; Germany withdraws from League of Nations; National Socialists achieve control of German government.

1934

Hitler becomes Germany's leader; Dionne quintuplets are born in Canada.

1935

Hitler renounces the Treaty of Versailles and begins openly rearming.

1936

Edward VII of England abdicates the throne, "for the woman I love"; Spanish Civil War begins.

1938

Remarque remarries Jutta so she will not be forced to return to Germany; Nazis take away his German citizenship; Germany annexes Austria; Hitler, Mussolini, Chamberlain (of Britain), and French premier sign Munich Pact for supposed mutual security.

1939

Remarque immigrates to United States; Germany annexes Czechoslovakia and invades Poland; World War II begins.

1941

Remarque becomes legal resident of the United States.

1943

December 16: Remarque's sister Elfriede Remark Scholz is beheaded by Nazis.

1945

United States uses atomic bomb against Japan; World War II ends; Hitler commits suicide; United Nations charter is signed in San Francisco.

1946

Nuremberg trials sentence Nazi war criminals.

1947

August: Remarque becomes naturalized American citizen; first supersonic flight; Dead Sea Scrolls discovered.

1948

Remarque returns to Switzerland; begins bicontinental life, living part-time in Switzerland and part-time in United States; state of Israel is established; Mahatma Gandhi, India's peace activist, is assassinated; civil war begins in Indochina (Vietnam).

1949

South Africa adopts apartheid as official policy; NATO is formed; Mao Tse-tung establishes a communist government in China; Germany is divided into East and West.

1953

Sir Edmund Hillary and Tensing Norgay are the first to climb Mount Everest.

1954

Remarque's father dies in Germany; United States gets involved in Vietnam; Russians launch *Sputnik*, starting the "Space Race."

1956

Hungarian Revolution.

1957

May: Remarque divorces Jutta again.

1958

February: Remarque marries American film actress Paulette Goddard.

1959

Fidel Castro overthrows Cuba's dictator, Juan Fulgencio Batista; microchip invented.

1961

Berlin Wall is erected; the Russian cosmonaut Yuri Gagarin becomes the first human in space.

1962

Telstar satellite is launched, enabling television transmission between the United States and Europe.

1963

U.S. president John F. Kennedy is assassinated.

1964

Remarque receives Justus Möser Medal from the German city of Osnabrück for distinguished and honored service.

1967

Remarque receives West Germany's Distinguished Service Cross of the Order of Merit; Israel's Six-Day War; first heart transplant is performed.

1968

Remarque is elected to German Academy for Language and Literature; Martin Luther King Jr. is assassinated.

1969

Neil Armstrong and Buzz Aldrin are the first men to land on the moon.

1970

September 25: Remarque dies of heart failure in St. Agnese Hospital, Locarno, Switzerland.

FOR FURTHER RESEARCH

ABOUT ERICH MARIA REMARQUE AND HIS WORKS

Christine R. Barker and R.W. Last, *Erich Maria Remarque.* London: Oswald Wolff, 1979. A study of Remarque and his works, with particular emphasis on *All Quiet.*

Richard Arthur Firda, All Quiet on the Western Front: *Literary Analysis and Cultural Context.* New York: Twayne, 1993. Good overview of Remarque's life and his best-known novel, *All Quiet on the Western Front,* as well as its adaptation to film.

Julie Gilbert, *Opposite Attraction.* New York: Pantheon, 1995. A dual biography of Remarque and actress Paulette Goddard, who became his wife.

C.R. Owen, *Erich Maria Remarque: A Critical Bio-Bibliography.* Amsterdam: Rodopi, 1984. Annotated descriptions of extensive collection of sources on Remarque, many of them German. Includes pertinent quotations.

Harley U. Taylor Jr., *Erich Maria Remarque: A Literary and Film Biography.* New York: Peter Lang, 1977. An easy-to-read study of Remarque and his works.

Hans Wagener, *Understanding Erich Maria Remarque.* Columbia: University of South Carolina Press, 1991. Brief but scholarly study of Remarque's works in the context of his life and times.

ABOUT REMARQUE AND *ALL QUIET*

Marlene Dietrich, *Marlene,* trans. Salvator Attanasio. New York: Grove Press, 1987. The famous actress's memoirs, not well written but interesting. Includes brief discussion of her friendship with Remarque.

Bruno Frei, ed., *The Stolen Republic: Selected Writings of Carl von Ossietzky.* London: Lawrence and Wishart, 1971. A collection of writings by one of the Weimar Republic's best-known journalists and social critics. Helps give a feel for the times as viewed by a loyal German who objected to Hitler and his ilk. Includes a short piece on Remarque.

Holger Klein, ed., *The First World War in Fiction: A Collection of Critical Essays.* New York: Barnes & Noble, 1976. These essays analyze many of the world's most prominent works of fiction relating to World War I, from John Dos Passos's *Three Soldiers* to Ernst Junger's *In Stahlgewittern.* Includes an essay on *All Quiet.*

Egbert Krispyn, *Anti-Nazi Writers in Exile.* Athens: University of Georgia Press, 1978. Whether by force or by personal desire, many writers fled Germany in the 1930s and 1940s. This book discusses the experiences of and works produced by several of these writers.

Edwin M. Moseley, *Pseudonyms of Christ in the Modern Novel: Motifs and Methods.* Philadelphia: University of Pittsburgh Press, 1962. Examines several novels in which the protagonist can be seen as a Christ figure. One chapter focuses on Paul Bäumer of *All Quiet.*

David Niven, *Bring on the Clowns.* New York: Putnam, 1975. The actor's memoirs. Includes mention of Remarque and his relationship with actress Paulette Goddard, who became his second wife.

William K. Pfeiler, *War and the German Mind: The Testimony of Men of Fiction Who Fought at the Front.* Morningside Heights, NY: Columbia University Press, 1941. Discusses novels written between 1919 and 1939 by former German soldiers. Includes brief section on Remarque.

Robert van Gelder, *Writers and Writing.* New York: Scribner, 1946. Collection of critic van Gelder's critical writing, including a short interview with Remarque.

ABOUT WORLD WAR I

Modris Eksteins, *Rites of Spring: The Great War and the Birth of the Modern Age.* Boston: Houghton Mifflin, 1989. Explores the impact of World War I on the generation that lived through it.

John Ellis, *Eye-Deep in Hell: Trench War in World War I.* Baltimore: Johns Hopkins University Press, 1976. Daily life in the trenches; includes photos and numerous brief excerpts from first-person accounts.

Martin Gilbert, *The First World War: A Complete History.* New York: Owl/Henry Holt, 1994. Detailed history covering all the fronts from beginning to end.

S.L.A. Marshall, *World War I.* Boston: Houghton Mifflin, 1992. A history by American brigadier general Marshall and the editors of *American Heritage.*

James L. Stokesbury, *A Short History of World War I.* New

York: William Morrow, 1981. A short, scholarly overview of all aspects of the war.

A.J.P. Taylor, *The First World War, an Illustrated History.* New York: Perigee, 1963. Compact history with numerous photos from official and private sources.

J.M. Winter, *The Experience of World War I.* New York: Oxford University Press, 1995. An illustrated history, filled with photos, illustrations, and diagrams as well as text.

SELECTED ARTICLES

A.F. Bance, *"Im Westen nichts Neues*: A Bestseller in Context," *Modern Language Review,* April 1977.

W. Duesberg, "Telephoning Remarque," *Living Age,* June, 1931.

Modris Eksteins, *"All Quiet on the Western Front,"* *History Today,* November 1995.

"Erich Maria Remarque, the Violent Author . . . a Quiet Man," *Newsweek,* April 1, 1957.

Roland Garrett, "Liberal Education on the Western Front," *Journal of General Education,* Fall 1979.

Frank Ernest Hill, "Destroyed by the War," *New York Herald Tribune,* June 2, 1929.

Charles W. Hoffmann, "Erich Maria Remarque," *German Fiction Writers, 1914–1945,* ed., James Hardin. Detroit: Gale Research, 1987.

"Im Westen nichts Neues," *American Mercury,* August 1929.

Bernard Kalb, "A Man of Peace and Plenty," *Saturday Review of Literature,* May 15, 1954.

Joseph Wood Krutch, "Glorious War," *Nation,* July 10, 1929.

Frédéric Lefèvre, "An Hour with Erich Remarque," *Living Age,* December 1930.

T.S. Matthews, "Bad News," *New Republic,* June 19, 1929.

"The Men Who Were Boys," *New Statesman,* May 25, 1929.

"Not All Quiet for Remarque," *Literary Digest,* October 12, 1929.

"Preferences," *Canadian Forum,* August 1929. Followed by reader correspondence in September and November 1929.

Herbert Read, "Books of the Quarter," *Criterion,* April 1929.

Erich Maria Remarque and Ian Hamilton, "The End of War? A Correspondence Between the author of *All Quiet on the Western Front* and General Sir Ian Hamilton, G.C.B., G.C.M.G." *Life and Letters,* vol. III, July/December 1929.

Mordecai Richler, "1944: The Year I Learned to Love a German," *New York Times Book Review*, February 2, 1986.

Jerold Simmons, "Film and International Politics: The Banning of *All Quiet on the Western Front* in Germany and Austria, 1930–1931," *Historian*, November 1989.

"Soldiers' Repartee, *Commonweal*, May 27, 1931.

M.J.V., "Social Fiction and Drama Notes," *Sociology and Social Research*, September/October 1929.

WORKS BY ERICH MARIA REMARQUE

Note: Remarque's first language was German. Most of his works were originally published in German and then translated to English. The list below gives the English title first, along with the original translator and first English-language publication date. The German titles with publication date are listed in parentheses. Besides novels, Remarque wrote numerous magazine articles, poems, and essays, and five plays. Thirteen feature films have been made from his works, including two versions of *All Quiet on the Western Front* (the acclaimed 1930 film starring Lew Ayres as Paul Bäumer, and the 1979 film made for television starring Richard Thomas).

The Dream Room, not published in English (*Die Traumbude: Ein Künstlerroman*, 1920)

All Quiet on the Western Front, trans. A.W. Wheen, 1929 (*Im Westen nichts Neues*, 1929)

The Road Back, trans. A.W. Wheen, 1931 (*Der Weg Züruck*, 1931)

Three Comrades, trans. A.W. Wheen, 1937 (*Drei Kameraden*, 1937)

Flotsam, trans. Denver Lindley, 1941 (*Liebe Deinen Nächsten*, 1941)

Arch of Triumph, trans. Walter Sorell and Denver Lindley, 1946 (*Arc de Triomphe*, 1946)

Spark of Life, trans. James Stern, 1952 (*Der funke Leben*, 1952)

A Time to Love and a Time to Die, trans. Denver Lindley, 1954 (*Zeit zu leben und Zeit zu sterben*, 1954)

The Black Obelisk, trans. Denver Lindley, 1957 (*Der schwarze Obelisk: Geschichte einer verspäteten*, 1956)

Heaven Has No Favorites, trans. Richard and Clara Winston, 1961 (*Der Himmel kennt keine Günstlinge*, 1961)

The Night in Lisbon, trans. Ralph Manheim, 1961 (*Die Nacht von Lissabon*, 1962)

Shadows in Paradise, trans. Ralph Manheim, 1972 (*Schatten im Paradies*, 1971)

INDEX